The Liturgical Context of Early European Drama

𝔖cripta 𝔥umanistica

Directed by
BRUNO M. DAMIANI
The Catholic University of America

ADVISORY BOARD

The Liturgical Context
of
Early European Drama

Salvatore Paterno

𝔖𝔠𝔯𝔦𝔭𝔱𝔞 𝔥𝔲𝔪𝔞𝔫𝔦𝔰𝔱𝔦𝔠𝔞

56

Paterno, Salvatore.
    The liturgical context of early European drama / Salvatore Paterno.
        p. cm. — (Scripta Humanistica ; 56)
    Bibliography : p.
    ISBN 0-916379-62-0 : +33.50
    1. Christian drama, Latin (Medieval and modern)—History and
criticism. 2. Catholic Church—Liturgy—Texts—History and
criticism. 3. Liturgical drama—History and criticism. 4. Drama.
Medieval—History and criticism. 5. Christianity and literature.
6. Liturgy and literature. I. Title. II. Series : Scripta
Humanistica (Series) ; 56.
PA8142.P38   1989   89-6256
264'.02'009015—dc20   CIP

Publisher and Distributor:
SCRIPTA HUMANISTICA
1383 Kersey Lane
Potomac, Maryland 20854 U.S.A.

Table of Contents

Preface   1
Foreword   3
Introduction   5

Chapter I   CHRISTIAN ATTITUDE IN A PAGAN MILIEU   7
    A. Patristic Period   8
        a. Tertullian   8
        b. Novation   8
        c. St. Cyprian of Carthage   9
        d. Lactantius   10
        e. St. John Chrysostom   11
        f. Salvian   12
        g. Ausonius   14
        h. St. Clement of Alexandria   16
        i. Appolinaris   17
        j. St. Athanasius   19
        k. Prudentius   21
        l. St. Augustine   23

Chapter II   ECCLESISTICAL, RESTRICTIONS AND
                PROHIBITIONS   25
    1. Synod   26
    2. Canons of the African Church   27
    3. Council of Trullo   28
    4. Council of Elvira   29
    5. Council of Toledo III   31

Chapter III NOTION OF WORSHIP: FROM TEXT TO
            PERFORMANCE   34
            1. Evidence from the Old Testament   35
            2. Evidence from the New Testament   37
            3. Evidence from the Christian Community   38

Chapter IV NATURE OF WORSHIP ENTAILS THE SENSE OF THE
            DRAMATIC   41
            Evidence of Dramatic Impulse In Early Liturgical
            Texts   42
                1. Pre-Nicene Period   42
                2. Post Nicene Period   45
                3. Pilgrimage of Egeria   60

Chapter V   RECONCILIATION OF PENITENTS   67
            1. Church's Position   67
            2. Old Testament Basis   68
            3. Patristic Period   69
            4. Development and Contents of the Rite for
                Penitents   72
            5. Penitential Gestures   74
            6. The Rite Itself   77
            7. Concluding Remark   81

Chapter VI DEDICATION OF CHURCHES   83
            1. Old Testament Sources   84
            2. Early Patristic Sources   85
            3. Later Christian Sources   88

Chapter VII CORONATION OF RULERS AND OF THOSE IN
            AUTHORITY   102
                1. Early Testimony   102
                2. Coronation Rites   103
                3. The Sanctuary   103
                4. Investing King with Insignia   104
                5. Anointing of the King   104
                6. Acclamations   105
                7. Royal Throne   105
                8. Homage   106

A. Dramatic Overtones of Biblical Texts   106
B. Early Evidence of Anointing   108
    a. St. Gregory   108
    b. Julian of Toledo   108
    c. Charlemagne   109
    d. Hincmar of Rheims   111
    e. Louis II   115
C. Anglo-Saxon England   116
    1. King Edgar   117
    2. Egbert's Pontifical   118
D. Continental Witnesses   120
    1. Aachen   120
    2. St. Peter Damian   121
    3. Papal Coronations   122

Chapter VIII   MONASTIC INFLUENCES   124
A. Divine Office   124
B. *Regularis Concordia*   125
C. Monastic Constitutions of Lanfranc   129
D. St. Hildegard of Bingen   135
E. Monastic Displeasure   138

Chapter IX   SUNDRY ELEMENTS OF DRAMATIC NATURE IN THE
    LITURGY   140
A. Eastern Testimony   140
B. Western Testimony   142
C. Hand Clapping   148
D. Vatican Council II   148

Conclusion   150
Bibliography   154

Preface

In *The Liturgical Context of Early European Drama,* Salvatore Paterno investigates broadly in time and space for his convincing argument that the Church which increasingly distanced herself from the mounting secular aspects of dramatic productions had really established a basis, stimulus and inspiration for the creation of a strong, independent genre, the theater. This major artistic endeavor thereby owes much of its substrata to the various liturgical elements of the early Middle Ages.

The sure decline of dramatic form after the triumph of the Church following Constantine's conversion was at times abetted indirectly and directly during the Christian centuries by religious forces which, however, were sowing the seeds simultaneously for the sources of a revival and renaissance of theatrical art. Paterno finds neither irony nor contradiction in these historical developments but rather a neglected ecclesiastical contribution to the world of the theater; and, indeed, he concludes that, without this important underpinning of rites, ceremonies and rituals, the field of drama would be lacking some fundamental drives and directions.

Notes and bibliography range from expected theological authorities to classical and modern references, such as Shakespeare, Frazer and Jung, plus some unexpected evidence in recent recordings of Abelard, the Plays of David, Daniel and Saint Nicholas among others, in order to enhance this overview of these dramatic influences. There are also a few sketches of the floor plans for religious events to illustrate a budding concept of staging and the place of the audience. Quotations are certainly utilized skillfully to render understandable the medieval feeling for dialogue and, of course, for the indispensable primary and critical support.

This broad survey initially traces the Christian presence in a pagan ambience from Tertullian to Augustine; then, the impact of two synods, canons of the African Church, and three Councils upon the theatrical tradition; the Biblical texts; and the growing Christian communities. A definitive trend in liturgical texts emerged in the dividing line between the pre- and post-Nicene periods when, by the latter time, an unmistakable movement can be gleamed toward a merger of a dramatic sense into the official Christian worship. Three uncommon examples provide a demonstration of Paterno's investigation in depth and are impressive for the exceptional quality of the liturgy: the reconciliation of penitents, the dedication of churches, and the coronation of rulers and of those in authority. Surprisingly, also, monastic disciplines are discussed as contributory to a theatrical mood as well as hand clapping being acceptable in some locales and the distinct variations of the Mozarabic liturgy in Spain.

This rich and varied heritage is likewise cited for the present-day Church whose liturgical reforms after the Second Vatican Council have come full circle in many ways with a return to the submerged precedents of earlier times, and this circular route breaks clearly more than once with ecclesiastical restrictions and prohibitions of the early Church. Both these developments are indicated by Paterno as an explanation and a justification of the abundant changes in form but obviously not in substance of the present-day Church.

This book can be interestingly and profitably read not only by an academic audience but also by a general public for an understanding and appreciation of two bedrocks, drama and liturgy, of twentieth-century culture.

Lawrence H. Klibbe
New York University

Foreword

This is an in-depth analysis of liturgical texts which constituted the basis for a dramatic output in the early Middle Ages. It is evident that the Church acted out a role as a cultural sponsor by supplying the liturgical texts and by nurturing the dramatic impulse which naturally associated itself with the texts. As a result, the liturgical texts and gestures served as a major thrust toward the surge of early drama.

The early period of the Christian era is portrayed as one which rigorously disapproved any sort of dramatic presentation. Ironically the church was supplying ample texts which indirectly became the nucleus of a dramatic force which was unleashed as time went on. The work is examines several liturgical sources and demonstrates how they definitely served as contributory factors to the development of early European drama.

The first of these major elements is the Church's liturgical setting for the reception of repentant sinners. The rite composed of Scriptural and Patristic texts, joined to the natural gestures of penance, developed into an impressive Rite of Reconciliation.

The Rite for the dedication of Churches is another interesting factor. Using Scripture and ritual, this rite demonstrates an elaborate and impressive ceremony. The assignment of prayers the function of the laity and the rubrics of the celebrant enhance a dramatic atmosphere. The climax seems to be reached in the Ceremony of the Alphabet.

The Coronation Rite of Rulers, if it does not coalesce, at least, it lends to a quasi-religious civil ceremony. The anointing of the regent and the presentation of the regalia by predominant members of the hierarchy manifests a dramatic and awesome presentation. The function of the clergy is parallel to the roles performed by major characters.

3

Attention is given to the impact which the monastic life-style had on the liturgy. The work analytically examines the festive texts employed for the celebration of many holy days and manifests the way in which they naturally lent themselves to a more dramatic presentation of monastic prayer since there was ample time, elaborate ceremony, and sufficient 'actors'.

The presence of unrecorded dramatic activity will be clearly attested to by the reconstruction of liturgical sources. As a consequence, this work will contribute to filling the gap prior to the *Quem Quaerites* to the period of actual dramatic documentation.

Introduction

Ancient World

The dance seems to have played a vital part in the religious life of many ancient peoples. Perhaps it began as mere ceremony or custom and eventually added with a religious tone, while in some societies it never received a religious significance. Although the dance is mentioned in connection with religious festivity in the Old Testament, it never really attained a place of importance. We read in *Exodus* 15:20-21:

> "The prophetess Miriam, Aaron's sister, took a tambourine in her hand, while all the women went out after her with tambourines, dancing; and she led them in the refrain:
> Sing to the Lord, for he is gloriously triumphant;
> horse and chariot he has cast into the sea."

The overall tone of this incident is one of joy and festivity. The people had been freed by the power of their God, and He had manifested to them His concern and care. There is rejoicing because that which has taken place delights the people, while at the same time some sort of praise is rendered by dance, to the Divinity. Several hundred years later David has the Ark placed on a new cart to be brought to Jerusalem. David made merry with all his strength, with singing and with cymbals. One reads in *II Samuel* 6:14, 16:19:

> "Then David, girt with a linen apron, came dancing before the Lord with abandon, as he and all the Israelites were bringing up the Ark of the Lord with shouts of joy and to the sound of the horn...Saul's

5

daughter Michal looked down through the window and saw King David leaping and dancing before the Lord...David offered holocausts and peace offerings before the Lord...he blesses the people then distributed among all the people, to each man and each woman in the entire multitude of Israel, a loaf of bread, a cut of roast meat, and a raisin cake. With this, all the people left for their homes."

Dance and celebration seem to recieve the game attention as the transferral of the Ark. It comes as no surprise to view this expression of worship in the Judeo-Christian tradition, i.e., both the spiritual as well as physical element in man have equal share in adoring the invisible God. The dance, in this context, although performed by David alone, retains its dignified expression of prayer. His dancing before the Lord, is the externalization of that same sentiment which he expresses in offering holocausts and peace offerings — the formalized pattern of prayer. For David, this dancing and making merry before the Lord, are truly expressions of adoration. The religious tone is not diminished by the mentioning of the distribution of bread, meat and raisin cake, on the contrary, it seems to intensify the overall well being that the worshipers experience after good liturgy, i.e., public worship.

On the other hand, the dance in the *Germania* of Tacitus (55-120 A.D.) is mentioned as a form of public show. There are no religious overtones connected with it. In Chapter 28, Tacitus relates that this form of public skill is sought by the youths of Germania. Trained in this barbarian tradition, naked youths dance with skill and grace at swords and spears that are aimed at them. They receive no money for the performance, but delight in the entertainment they afford the onlookers. The dance is mainly an expression of skill and a means of recreation.

In the above accounts, we are presented with the treatment of the dance — perhaps man's earliest manifestation of a desire to dramatize, by two ancient cultures; in Germanic culture, the dance remains an expression of skill. Both examples seem to indicate the fact, that man wishes to bodily express certain actions so as to create a mood or emotion, and to bring to the surface that inner sentiment that can be perceived by action alone.

6

I
Christian Attitude in a Pagan Milieu

According to our Christian standards of today, the austere and rigorous lifestyle demanded for the Christian in the early days of the Church, would seem rather too ascetic or even fanatical. One must remember that martyrdom was very real for the early Christians, and their disciplined behavior was almost taken for granted. When it came to means of entertainment, however, as harmless as some of them seemed, they too were forbidden to the Christians. The demand placed upon Christians, which forbade them public shows, was initiated primarily because these shows or games were presented on some pagan feast day, hence, the performance was in some way related to pagan religion. Christians were also barred from such entertainment because violence, evil, cruelty and lewd conduct could easily be viewed by the spectators. As simple an activity as a horse race could have easily produced a mob scene, bloodshed, and even death. Nevertheless, Christians did attend such spectacles; the renunciation of the world they made at baptism was not so easy to maintain. For the next few centuries, the Christian was exhorted to separate the theatre — the devil's instrument — from Christian life. Several early Christian writers tackled the question: "Is it proper for Christians to attend these shows?" The amphitheatre itself provided the area for all types of entertainment: stage, performances, wrestling, horse racing, and mimes and dancers.

A.   Christian Writers Rigorously Opposed to the Spectacles

   1.   *Tertullian*, 160-220 A.D.

Tertullian's work *De Spectaculis*[1] contains his zealous presentations and harsh treatment toward the laxity so prevalent among some Christians, especially among those who attended the public shows. The reason he gives to Christians for not being permitted to attend public spectacles is that they are associated with pagan worship and they arouse passion. His fiery presentation conveys the sense of betrayal, the shows are the enemies' camp, the place where immodesty, rage, fighting and grief are nurtured. Any sense of pretense is frowned upon. This would make it rather difficult when acting out someone's age, emotion, or sex. As for character dress, he reminds those who dress for female roles to reconsider after reading God's word in Deut. 22:5. To those who attend these shows for purely literary delight, Tertullian advises them to take pleasure in reading more edifying and religious works as found in the Scriptures. There, he suggests, one finds reality. Attendance at these shows was surely a sign of laxity, and play into the devil's hand. Such behavior was not compatible with Christian beliefs. It would come as no surprise that Tertullian frowned even upon the notion of pantomime.

   2.   *Novatian* (C.200 -?)

Novatian, a priest of Rome, was a rigorist as was Tertullian of North Africa. It is evident that Novatian was inspired to write his own *Spectacles* after reading Tertullian's work. The theme runs parallel to Tertullian's — the Christian should not attend these places of amusements. Very emphatically Novatian condemns the Christian for attending these spectacles. He states that idolatry is the mother of all these games.[2] No doubt many Christians argued with him on the issue of reading about musical instruments,[3] boxing

---

[1]   Written in 197 A.D.

[2]   Novatian, *De Spectaculis*, Ch. 4.

[3]   2 Kings 6:4

and wrestling[4] against the devil, and even the notion of the garland[5] as a prize, all taken from Scripture. Novatian comments:

> "These things were written to incite our minds to greater enthusiasm for salutary things..."[6]

What is interesting to note is the fact that he does mention tragedy and comedy, alas, he has no use for them as literary expressions at all.

> "Why should I even mention the wasted efforts of comedy and those senseless ravings of the tragic voice?"[7]

Novatian exhorts the Christian to take delight in God's creation, and in the beauty of the Christian Faith. Interesting for the reader is the fact that the genre of tragedy and comedy is mentioned. This indicates as to what literary work was staged in the ancient theatre, and that the people's entertainment did not consist in games alone. Moreover, Novatian considers it unthinkable for a Christian to stop at the theatre on his way home after attending the Eucharist; what makes matters worse is the fact that some believers had the Eucharist on their persons so that during the week they may communicate themselves at home. This bit of information gives us an historical account of the ancient practice of the Eucharist being brought home by the laity.

3. *St. Cyprian, Bishop of Carthage*, C. 200-258 A.D.

Cyprian became Bishop of Carthage in 248 A.D., living in an atmosphere of persecution. He was martyred in 258 A.D. His writings portray him as a prudent, charming, and skilled administrator. His firmness never turns into harshness of rigorism. Nevertheless, his personal touch exemplified in his writings, does not prevent his condemning his flock for attending public amusements. He asks what is the Christian doing there in the first place.[8] Horse racing, wrestling and senseless jokes can easily become a vice for the spectator. Besides, if there is any indication of idolatry, the Christian

---

[4]   Eph 6:12; 1 Cor 9:26
[5]   1 Cor 9:24
[6]   Novatian, *De Spectaculis*, Ch. 2.
[7]   *Ibid.*, Ch. 7.
[8]   St. Cyprian. *Ad Donatum.*

9

should even more so shun these places. He concludes with the same admonition as given by Novatian-natural wonders, wrought by the hand of God, and the revealing of God's love for man, found in the Scriptures, should be the source and cause for the Christians' delight.

4. *Lactantius* C. 250-330 A.D.

Lactantius is another literary figure from North Africa, who became a Christian in 303 A.D. His graceful style won for him the title of the Christian Cicero. Pico della Mirandola and other humanists called him so.[9] In his work, *Divine Institutes,* Bk. VI, Ch. 20, Lactantius claims that the comedies and tragedies viewed on stage are a disgraceful presentation of gestures which can become occasions of sin for the viewer, young or old. The mime and his staging should be avoided. There is the possibility present, that a pagan god may be honored at one of these presentations, hence, for the Christian, attendance at these affairs could be considered a departure from the worship of God and a return to corruption. This certainly is taking a step backward in the spiritual life.

Again we are given the ingredients of what the theatre was made up of at that time. The mimes must have had an equally prominent position on the list of entertainment, for Lactantius calls for their being shunned; they too excite vice. One notices in these admonitions, a lack of rigorism or ultra ascetical tone. However there remains the sharp plea for the Christian to remain true to his faith and not think of attending these amusements. In a very reasonable way, Lactantius states his position, which is that the theatre will demoralize the Christian, then in a very logical presentation, presents the reasons with which the Christian would have to agree to with an honest and intelligible response. This selection will demonstrate his lucidity:

> For the subject of comedies are the dishonouring of young girls, or the loves of harlots; and the more eloquent they are who have composed the accounts of these disgraceful actions, the more do they persuade by the elegance of their sentiments; and harmonious and polished verses more readily remain fixed in the memory of the hearers. In like manner, the stories of the tragedians place before the eyes and parricides and incests of wicked kings, and represent tragic crimes.

---

9   Patrick J. Hamell, *Handbook of Patrology*, p. 78.

10

And what other effect do immodest gestures of the players produce, but both teach and excite lusts whose enervated bodies, rendered effeminate after the gait and dress of women, imitate unchaste women by their disgraceful gestures. Why should I speak of the actors of mimes, who hold forth instruction in corrupting influences, who teach adulteries while they feign them, and by pretended actions train to those which are true? What can young men or young girls do, when they see these things practiced without shame, and willingly beheld all? They are plainly admonished of what they can do, and are inflamed with lust, which is especially excited by seeing...And they approve of these things, while they laugh at them, and with vices clinging to them, they return more corrupted to their apartments; and not boys only, who ought not to be inured to vices prematurely, but also old men, whom it does not become at their age to sin... Therefore all spectacles ought to be avoided, not only that no vice may settle on our breasts, which ought to be tranquil and peaceful; but that the habitual indulgence of any pleasure may not soothe and captivate us, and turn us aside from God and from good works. For the celebrations of the games are festivals in honour of the gods, inasmuch as they were instituted on account of their birthdays, or the dedication of new temples... Therefore, if any one is present at the spectacles to which men assemble for the sake of religion, he has departed from the worship of God, and has betaken himself to those deities whose birthdays and festivals he has celebrated.

5. *St. John Chrysostom* C. 347-407 A.D.

Attendance at shows was equally frowned upon by the bishops in the Eastern sector of the Empire. John was born in Antioch, and at an early age gratified his teachers with the promise of his learning. When he was ordained priest in 386, his chief duty was to be the preacher at the main church in Antioch. There he preached his famous sermons for almost twelve years. His reputation spread throughout the whole East while his authority as orator, exegete, essayist and educationalist was not without a mighty impact. Several years after his death, the surname "Golden-mouthed" was affixed to his name. Now he, too, launched out against those Christians who were lax in selecting their form of entertainment. In his Homily XV, Chapter 11,[10] delivered from the church pulpit in Antioch, John makes it quite clear that theatre going has no place in the life of the Christian. He warns his flock that such behavior is exposing the Christian to trouble, temptation and to an extent, mental anguish. The theatre is to be avoided as an occasion of sin. The Christian cannot afford to take a risk of placing himself in a situation which would lead to fornication and intemperance. It must be kept in mind, that the renunciation of the evil made in baptism was to be lived in such a dynamic union with Christ, that to make a rift from Him or from his message would seem almost unthinkable. The impending threat of martyrdom during the early centuries of the Church contributed to this overall atmosphere of moral austerity. Other Christian writers[11] of that era zealously condemn such entertainment and make a plea for strict ethical standards.

6. *Salvian*, C. 400-470 A.D.

Surprisingly enough, one finds Christian writers of the fifth century advocating the avoidance of the theatre. A rigorist, sort of reformer and moralist was the writer Salvian of Marseille. His writings reveal him as a preacher instilling into his congregation the fact that the Almighty punishes the evil doer in this present life. He seems harsh toward the Christians for their failings while he flatters the barbarian. One of the evils to be abhorred by all Christians is attendance at the theatre. In his work: *The Governance of God*,[12] he cynically reprimands his audience with these words found in Book VI, Chapters 6-6:

> In the games thee is a certain apostasy from the faith and a deadly deviation from the Creed and from the heavenly pledges. For, what is the first confession of faith of Christians in the saving baptism? What is it except that they profess they are renouncing the devil, his pomps

---

[10]   NICENE and POST NICENE Fathers, Vol. IX, p. 442.

[11]   Tatian, d. 173 A.D., Clement of Alexandria, 150 - 215 A.D., Minucius Felix, d.c. 250, Origen, 185-254 A.D.

[12]   *DeGubernatione Dei, Salvian the Priest of Marseilles*, Jeremiah F. O'Sullivan, Ph.D., Cima Publishing Company New York, NY 1947. *New Catholic Encyclopedia*, Vol. 12, McGraw Hill, New York, Also *Catholic Historical Review*, January 1982, article on Salvian.

and games and works. Therefore, according to our profession of faith, the games and pomps are the work of the devil.

How, therefore, O Christians, do you frequent the games after baptism, the games which you confess to be the work of the devil? You have once renounced the devil and his games. You must know that when you return to the games you are returning knowingly and deliberately to the devil. For you have renounced both things, and at the same time you have said one is both. If you return to one, you resort to both. You say, I renounce the devil, his pomps, spectacles and works'.

Again, therefore, I must return to what I have often said: What is there like this among barbarians? Where among them are there circuses, where are there theatres, where the crime of different impurities; that is to say, the ruin of our hope and salvation?

Where, therefore, is our Christianity, we who receive the sacrament of salvation only for the purpose that we may sin afterwards with the greater crime of deviation from righteousness? We prefer stage plays to the churches of God. We spurn the altars and honor the theatres. We love things and worship things. God alone, in comparison with all other things, is vile to us.

I ask of everybody's conscience what place has greater crowds of Christian men: the spectators' benches at the public games or the entrance to the house of God? Do the crowds prefer the temple or the theatre? Do they love more the teachings of the Gospel; or the theatrical musicians; the words of life or the words of death; the words of Christ or the words of the mime?

There is no doubt that we love more that which we prefer. For, on every day of the fatal games whatever feast of the Church it may be, not only do those who say they are Christians not come to the church, but, if any come perhaps unwittingly, if they hear the games being performed, while they are already in the church, they leave the church... The devil is in his spectacles and in his pomps. Therefore, when we return to the spectacles of the devil, we forsake the faith of Christ. In this way, all pledges of our faith are broken.

Not all Christian writers wrote in such a tone. Salvian, emphasizes the relentless wrath of God in this life.

B. Christian Writer *Less* Rigorously Opposed to the Spectacles

1. *Decimus Magnus Ausonius,* C. 310-395

Among the many delightful writers of that period is Decimus Magnus Ausonius, C. 310-395. a doctor's son, who was born at Bordeaux (Burdigala). He pursued his studies in rhetoric and eventually became the founder of the University of Bordeaux in 334. St. Paulinus who afterwards became the bishop of Nola in Italy was a pupil as well as a close friend. Ausonius seems to have been some type of nonchalant Christian himself. Of all the ancient writers, Ausonius, no doubt, would fit in comfortably with our Romantic writers. In his work *Ludus Septem Sapientum,*[13] found in Book VIII, *Masque of the Seven Sages,* the reader will find it very interesting to sense the tone of this almost comic presentation. The witty arrangement of seven classical sages, who are persuaded to appear on stage to deliver their own wise saying with a humorous speech encourage the audience for its application in their own daily life. Here there is no acting as such or drama, but what makes Ausonius' work relevant is the appearance of the words: stage (scaena) and orchestra (orchestra). Moreover, the invitation of the speaker for applause at the end of his own speech is very much like an epilogue found in some Shakespearean plays, though not as lengthy.[14] It is evident that the idea of a theatre was still alive in that area of Europe, where one would tend to think the atmosphere was more tolerant toward the idea of theatre. After reading the works of Ausonius, one would have to agree that Ausonius had neither scruples when it came to theatre, nor would one think he was rigorous in advocating the idea of shunning the theatre. The following selections of *The Masque of the Seven Sages*[15] will give a fair idea of the style Ausonius employs.

Their usage is to deliver their own sayings, each that which he in his wisdom first hit upon. You know, of course, what these are; but if Memory limps among ancient matters, Chorus will come fully to explain these sayings on which I have too slight a grip...with him all the rest of his life. Two kings bare witness in my praise, and both proved

---

[13] Hugh G. White, *Ausonius*, Vol I, Loeb Classical Library Series, Harvard University Press, Cambridge, Massachusetts, 1968.

[14] cf. Shakespeare's: *The Tempest,* Epilogue spoken by Prospero; *As You Like It,* Epilogue spoken by Rosalind; *All's Well That Ends Well; King Henry the Eight.*

[15] *Ausonius,* op. cit., pp. 310-329.

me right. And what was said to one, that let each consider spoken to himself.

Now I have finished that for which I came forward here. Look! Chilon is coming. Fare ye well and applaud.

—Chilon—

"My loins ache with sitting, my eyes with watching, while I waited" for Solon "to come to himself". Good Lord! What "brief speaking" these Athenians use! When at last he has finished off a single saw in heaven knows how many lines, he goes off looking back at me regretfully.

I have done: farewell, be thoughtful, I do not wait for applause"...

I accepted and dedicated it to Apollo; for if Phoebus bids the Wise One be chosen, "tis fitting to believe that not any man but a god is meant.

That man, then, am I. But the reason for my appearing on the stage, as with the two who have preceded me, is to become the champion of my own maxim. It will offend some, but not those canny ones who have learned from experience and have been made worldlywise.

...let each of you "mention such to himself and reflect how many have suffered loss and harm by standing surety. Yet may both parties still find pleasure in this service!

Clap, then, some of you; the rest, affronted, hiss me off the stage.

...So now that hated epithet "the bad" takes flight.

I must move off. Farewell and applaud, you who "most are good."

...Reflect, all of you, how often a man gets into trouble who has not watched for the right opportunity.

Time warns me not to be wearisome. Give me your applause.

The work concludes with the comments of Periander:

...There is nothing which can demand greater attention than to think what ought to be done. Therefore 'tis chance, not design, which governs the unreflecting.

But now I must rejoin my fellowcharacters. Applaud, and take thought while you manage your state affairs.

2. *Clement of Alexandria* 150-215 A.D.

It would be unfair to presume that no early church writer spoke favorably about drama at all. Well, without direct or indirect praise of drama, Clement of Alexandria mentions a drama in his work.[16] What makes this observation so interesting is the fact that the drama *The Exodus* was written by 'Ezekiel', a Hellenistic Jew, probably from Alexandria. From the evidence of the work's relationship to the Septuagint,[17] we can conclude *The Exodus*[18] was written not earlier than the beginning of the second century. In the 269 verses of iambic trimeters, the author wished to dramatize the events of Exodus as recorded in the Scriptures. Here, one would believe, surely we have a pre-Christian instance of text to performance. We would not be doing injustice to our imagination by considering this drama as a distant ancestor of the medieval religious plays. For Clement's adding these verses in his section on the life of Moses, would indicate that the play was tolerated then in Jewish circles as well as reading of whatever remained of it, in Christian circles. Interestingly enough, Clement has the section which begins with the soliloquy by Moses:

'And respecting the education of Moses, we shall find a harmonious account in Ezekiel, the composer of Jewish tragedies in the drama entitled *T he Exodus*. He thus writes in the person of Moses:

"For, seeing our race abundantly increase,
His treacherous snares King Pharaoh 'gainst us laid,
And cruelly in brick-kilns some of us,
And some, in toilsome works of building, plagues.
And towns and towers by toil of ill-starred men
He raised. Then to the Hebrew race proclaimed,
That each male child should in deepflowing Nile
Be drowned. My mother bore and hid me then
Three months (so afterwards she told). Then took,
And me adorned with fair array, and placed

---

[16] *Stromata* 1,23. Rev. Alex Roberts, *The Ante Nicene Fathers*, Vol. II, Charles Scribner's Sons, New York 1980, pp. 335-336.

[17] Earliest Greek translation of the Old Testament from original Hebrew — 2nd Century B.C., version used by the early Church.

[18] *Encyclopedia Judaica*, Vol. 6, Macmillan Company, New York, 1971, pp. 1102-1103.

On the deep sedgy marsh by Nilus bank,
While Miriam, my sister, watched afar.
Then, with her maids, the daughter of the king,
To bathe her beauty in the cleansing stream,
      ...And my name
Moses she called, because she drew and saved
Me from the waters on the river's bank.
And when the days of childhood had flown by,
My mother brought me to the palace where
The princess dwelt, after disclosing all
About my ancestry, and God's great gifts.
In boyhood's years I royal nurture had,
An in all princely exercise was trained,
As if the princess's very son. But when
The circling days had run their course,
I left the royal palace."

Then, after relating the combat between the Hebrew and the Egyptian, and the burying of the Egyptian in the sand, he says of the other contest:

"Why strike one feebler than thyself?
And he rejoined: Who made the judge o'er us,
Or ruler? Wilt thou slay me, as thou didst
Him yesterday? And I in terror said,
How is this known?"

Then he fled from Egypt and fed sheep, continues Clement. How familiar the style! Perhaps such plays were to entice the Jews away from pagan Gentile mundane plays, by presenting them their own religious history as a source of entertainment and leaving, a counterpart of which never really existed in the early Christian community. In any event, we can admit that there is evidence in the ancient world of the Scriptural text being the source of dramatic performance!

3. *Apollinaris of Laodicea,* C. 310-390 A.D.

It appears that a similar handling of Scripture was done later on by a Christian, Apollinaris of Laodicea, Syria. He was a close friend of St.

Athanasius. We learn that he was a famous teacher combining the polish of the classical world with his own talents and teaching ability. St. Jerome was one of his pupils at Antioch in 374.[19] Some Church historians[20] reveal interesting facts about his literary talent and skill, and the end product when both were made to function together. We read in Sozomen's account that when Emperor Julian prevented Christian children from attending public schools in 362, lest they be exposed to Greek literature, Apollinaris and his father composed comedies, tragedies and epics using the Bible as their primary source; by so doing, the pupils were at least exposed to the various genres employed by the Greeks. To reap these literary benefits:

> "...Apollinarist therefore employed his great learning and ingenuity in the production of a heroic epic on the antiquities of the Hebrews to the reign of Saul, as a substitute for the poem of Homer. He divided this work into twenty-four parts, to each of which he appended the name of one of the letters of the Greek alphabet, according to their number and order. He also wrote comedies in imitation of Menander, tragedies resembling those of Europides, and odes on the model of Pindar. In short, taking themes of the entire circle of knowledge from the Scriptures, he produced within a very brief space of time, a set of works which in manner, expression, character and arrangement are well approved as similar to the Greek literature."[21]

We even learn from the church historian, Socrates,[22] that Apollinaris used the Gospel for his inspiration to compose dialogues, very much like the ones written by Plato.

> ...The younger Apollinaris who was well trained in eloquence, expounded the gospels and apostolic doctrines in the way of dialogue, as Plato among the Greeks had done. Thus showing themselves useful to the Christian cause they overcame the subtlety of the emperor through their own labors.

---

[19] Cf. St. Jerome, Letter 84.
[20] Johannes Quasten, *Patrology*, Vol. III, pp. 377-381, Newman Press, MD, 1960.
[21] Sozomen, *Ecclesiastical History*, Bk. V, Chap. 18, *Nicene and Post Nicene Fathers*, Vol. II, Philip Schaff.
[22] Socrates, *Ecclesiastical History*, Bk. III, Chap. 16, *Nicene and Post Nicene Fathers*, Vol. II, Philip Schaff.

We read that his father, Apollinaris senior

> ...a grammarian composed a grammar consistent with the Christian
> faith: he also translated the Books of Moses into heroic verse; and
> phrased all the historical books of the Old Testament, putting them
> partly into dactylic measure, and partly reducing them to the form of
> dramatic tragedy. He purposely employed all kinds of verse, that no
> form of expression peculiar to the Greek language might be unknown
> or unheard of amongst Christians.

4. St. Athanasius, 295-373 A.D.

Another interesting writer and theologian, who escorts us into the library
atmosphere of his period, is *St. Athanasius*,[23] who gives us insights as to
how literary techniques were used by opponents in theological disputes. For
our purposes we will discuss one of Arius' works — a drama, *Thalia*, as
Athanasius writes in his work *De Sententia Dionysii*, Ch. 6:

> ...And while Arius to expound his own error wrote a Thalia in an ef-
> feminate and ridiculous style like Sotades the Egyptian,..

For Sotades, the Greek text reads corruptly Sosates. The name *Thalia*,
usually was associated with convivial songs. The meter of the fragments is
rather obscure. The lines seem to be composed of very corrupt anapestic
tetrameters, catalectic, as in a comic *Parabasis*.[24] Now in Discourse I,
Chapter II Athanasius tells us in sample form:

> Now the commencement of Arius's *Thalia* and flippancy, ef-
> feminate in tune and nature, runs thus:—

> 'According to faith of God's elect, God's prudent ones,
> Holy children, rightly dividing, God's Holy Spirit receiving,
> Have I learned this from the partakers of wisdom,

---

[23] He was born in Alexandria, Egypt; as a deacon he accompanied his bishop
to the Council of Nicea, 325 A.D. There he proved to be a vibrant opponent to
Arianism, the heresy that denied the divinity of Christ. Athanasius is very much aware
of how the heretic Arius uses literature to propagate his false teachings.

[24] Schaff and Wace, *Nicene and Post Nicene Fathers*, Vol. II, p. 457.

Accomplished, divinely taught, and wise in all things,
Along their track, have I been walking, with like opinions.
I the very famous, the much suffering for God's glory;
And taught of God, I have acquired wisdom and knowledge.'

And the mockeries which he utters in it, repulsive and most irreligious, are such as these: —'God was not always a Father;' but
'once God was alone, and not yet a Father, but afterwards He became
a Father.' 'The Son was not always;' for, whereas all things were made
out of nothing, and all existing creatures and works were made, so the
Word of God Himself was 'made out of nothing', and 'once He was
not,' and..[25]

After reading the extracts, the reader realizes why Athanasius became so in-
dignant, and was almost forced to admit:

Who is there that hears all this, nay, the tune of *Thalia*, but must
hate, and justly hate, this Arius jesting on such matters as on a stage?
Who but must regard him, when he pretends to name God and speak
of God but as a serpent...who, on reading what follows in his work,
but must discern in his irreligious doctrine that error, into which by his
sophistries the serpent in the sequel seduced the woman? Who at such
blasphemies is not transported?[26]

Arius' work, *Thalia* must have become famous and enjoyed a bit of suc-
cess otherwise Athanasius would not have been so vexed by it. Perhaps the
melodies were familiar and popular, what was so nefarious was the manner
in which Arius used these melodies and gestures to propagate his heresy.

There have been some studies made as to consider *Thalia* as a drama as
such. We may find their consideration quite interesting, without favoring any
position, the fact of their presence in early church history is revealing.

In stating her theory of the origins and development of the Byzantine
theatre, Mme. Cottas presents her opinion:

... Second period: The Church uses the popular profane theater
and the mime 'pour combattre les partisans de l'ancienne religion,

---

[25] Op. cit,. p. 308.
[26] Op. cit., p. 309.

comme aussi ceux des differentes heresies' (p.34). This happened especially during the Arian controversy. Arius gathered from the theaters and the streets profane rhythms and love melodies, and adapted them to words and poems written for theological propaganda. The orthodox party opposed to Arius' *Thalia* another work of the same type, the *Anti-Thalia*, and thus 'la gesticulation mimique' which was an essential part of the music and songs of the popular theater and the mime, was adopted also by the Church in its offices and in all its liturgical performances.[27]

In the article: *The Christos Paschon and the Byzantine Theater*,[28] Sandro Sticca maintains that Athanasius is referring to Arius "as if he were an histrio or pantomimus who gave imitation of human things and stories rather than a legitimate playwright." Whatever view is favored, one must admit that some amount of performance was in direct relation to a text!

5. *Prudentius*, 348-405 A.D.

Aurelius Clemens Prudentius (v. 348 A.D. Saragossa, Spain — d. after 405 A.D.), a layman like Ausonius, however more articulate in professing his belief; he stands for all that Arius opposed. Prudentius originated the Christian ode and Christian allegory, both devices were to have an influence in the literature of Medieval Europe.[29] His *Peristephanon* (The Martyrs' Crowns) should interest us. The work consists of hymns in praise of the martyrs, one of which depicts the dramatic pagan ritual — "taurobolium'; he vividly describes this rite which was associated with the worship of Cybele. Prudentius has the martyr, Romanus address his pagan persecutors:

'Your high priest verily goes down into a trench,
Dug deep beneath the earth, to there be sanctified,
With strange head band and festal chaplets on his brow.
His perfumed hair restrained beneath a golden crown
And Gabine cincture holding up his silken robe.

---

[27] *Speculum XI*, The Byzantine Theatre, p. 190, Medieval Academy of America, Cambridge, Mass. 1936.

[28] *Comparative Drama*, 8 (1974), pp. 13-44.

[29] Sister Clement Eagan, *The Poems of Prudentius*, p. XXIII, The Catholic University Press, 1962.

'Above the trench they build a platform made of planks.
Laid side by side with ample crevices between,
And then by cutting or by boring through the floor
They make a score of little openings in the wood.
'Then to the place is led a bull of monstrous size,
A flowery garland forms
A wreath around his shoulders and entwines his horns.
...glowing metal plates adorn his bushy hair.

'Above the trench the beast of sacrifice is placed.
With consecrated spear they open wide his heart,
And from the wound a stream of hot blood gushes out,
Which falls upon the bridge of wooden planks below
And spreads out over it, a heated billowing flood.
...'It filters in a gory shower of fetid rain
That falls upon the high priest in the pit below.
He holds his abject head to catch the dripping blood
That stains his robe and all his body with its filth.

'And leaning back, he lifts his cheeks to meet the spray,
Beneath it holds his ears, his nostrils and his lips,....

...'When all the blood is spent, the flamens drag away
The bullock's rigid carcass from the bridge of planks,
And frightful to behold, the pontiff then comes forth,
With dripping head and beard all matted by the clots,
His fillets sodden and his vestments drenched with blood.

'This man defiled by such impurity and filth,
Bespattered with the gore of recent sacrifice,
The crowd with reverential awe salutes and glorifies,
Because they think a dead ox's blood has hallowed him
As he was crouching in that dreadful cave below.[30]

The reader can easily visualize the clothing of the pagan priest, his stage apparel as it were, the action is vividly presented in detail. It is as though Prudentius opened the window of time and we peer into it and become the

---

[30]   Op. cit., pp. 234-235.

audience of this drama. It is not difficult to leave to our imaginations the context of the crowd's awesome acclamations and shouts of glory.

6. St. Augustine, 345-430 A.D.

To conclude she era in which the early Christians were prohibited from attending the decadent theatrical shows, it would be remiss to exclude the position of the theatre in the works of St. Augustine of Hippo. The Western World's heritage was menaced ever more so by the Barbarian threats. Fortunately, St. Augustine is one of the links in the chain between the ancient world and the Middle Ages. His writings, presented with such clarity and precision became the literary fountain or source for theologians and philosophers of later centuries.[31] He was the blossom of what went before, as it were, and the seed of what was to come. The style and construction found in the writings of St. Augustine contributed to his genius and dynamic influence. Indeed, it is no wonder that Charlemagne took great delight in his works, especially in The City of God.[32]

What quickly becomes evident in St. Augustine's treatment of the theatrical shows is his calm and less rigorous tone in renouncing them. His opposition to them underlies his serene style and tact, relying on common sense and arguing from reason rather than enforcing a pulpit oratory type presentation. His arguments appeal to the reader's intellect, who in turn, has the duty to form a self evident conclusion and act it through. His whole tone seems to be summed up in his very words.

"Listen to me, if your minds allow you to think sensibly".[33]

Further on he considers the craze for the theatre a disease that effects one's character. It is amazing to read his section which lacks all vigor rather one senses a tone of toleration:

"There are more acceptable dramatic compositions, namely comedies

---

[31] It was with the writing of St. Thomas Aquinas (1225-1274) that Western philosophy shifted from Platonic to Aristotelian, and with that, philosophy became the handmaid to theology. Previously there was no clear distinction between philosophy and theology.

[32]Einhard and Nother, Two Lives of Charlemagne, p. 78.

[33] City of God, Book I, Ch. 32, St. Augustine.

and tragedies poetical fictions designed for production in public shows. Their subject matter is often immoral, as far as action goes, but unlike many other compositions, they are at least free from verbal obscenities, and the older generations compel the young to read and learn them as part of what is called a liberal education for gentlemen."[34]

Knowing St. Augustine as an educationalist, one may easily conclude that he would have allowed theatre study for educational purposes. Unlike the other Christian writers, St. Augustine mentions Cicero, and not surprisingly at all, he mentions Plato as well.[35] While the names of other pagan writers seem to flow freely from his pen, other ancient writers would have deemed it less praiseworthy to mention them in their texts dealing with the same subject. Can one conclude then that the shows were more tolerated at this period of church history? The answer would be negative, because later the Christian attitude and local church councils would still carry the tone of prohibition. The fact is that St. Augustine writes in such a sophisticated way as to praise the art form but condemns the evil portrayed through a legitimate vehicle. What must be remembered is the fact that St. Augustine, as a Christian in faith is a Platonist in philosophy, and for him the battle between the flesh and the spirit continues.

---

[34] Op. cit., Chap. 8.
[35] Op. cit., Book VIII, Ch. 13.

II
Ecclesiastical Restrictions
and Prohibitions

One observation that is striking is the fact that a Scriptural source functioned as material for a pre-Christian era play, whereas similar resources were available in the Christian era, and from the information recorded, we gather dramas containing religious elements were performed, however for the Christian the theatre always remained an alien and somewhat foreign environment. The theatre was also considered a carry over from paganism, retaining many features which had their origin in pagan society. No wonder it was rather difficult for the Christian artist to put a Christian message in a pagan art form. It has been seen, however, that it was accomplished and accepted with very little enthusiasm. In no way did it seem to win popularity as did Ezekiel's *Exodus*.[36] An overall impression is had that the Church authorities and theologians are waging a sort of 'tug of war' with the performers or producers of dramatical works. Some areas of the empire and some periods of time indicate a relaxation of the prohibitions, a toleration to some degree and a passive acceptance of the fact that there were Christians attending the theatre. One must keep in mind that there was never a blending of the two, i.e. church and theatre, as such. The theatre was always considered a child of the pagan world and there could never be an acceptance, or blending of the two warehouses of art — the Church and the theatre. The very mention of theatre, during that early church period would conjure up the idea of Satan's territory or domain. The very word 'actor' or 'actress'

---

[36] cf. above Ezeckiel of Alexandria.

would imply a lewd type of individual. It would be inconceivable then to have even hoped for the two to have mutual admiration.

1 *Synod of Arles*, 314 A.D.

The bishops who attended this synod, fifty five miles northwest of Marseilles, formulated several canons of excommunication. Canon IV states that jockeys are excommunicated, Canon V adds *actors* to it. Both are on par with gladiatorial combats.[37]

2. *Synod of Laodicea*, 343-381 A.D

This was the city in Phrygia to which the early bishops met for a regional synod. The many disciplinary problems in church matters prompted them to issue several canons. For our information, Canon XV stated that: "No others shall sing in the church, save only the canonical singers, who go up to the ambo and sing from a book."[38]

In the local directives of Timothy of Alexandria (ob. 385 A.D.) we read Canon XXXIII: Actors and apostates were not to be refused reconciliation if they desire to return to the Church."[39]

Just by the joining of the word 'actors' to the word apostates one gets the sense of the low esteem directed toward actors. These disciplines seem rudimentary yet they were stern. The Church, at that time, was small in membership and the members were select, in such circumstances the discretion of the bishop, or bishops was final.

Nowhere were councils more frequent, in those early days, than in North Africa. Many of those synods were held at Carthage. What would happen was that previous Canons were again included into the new listing of canons, thereby resulting in an almost repetitious listing of familiar restrictions.

---

[37] R. T. Haslehurst, *Penitential Discipline in the Early Church*, p. 137, Mac-Millan, London, 1921.

[38] Philip Schaff, D.D., *Nicene and Post Nicene Fathers*, Vol. 14, p. 132, Charles Scribner's Sons, New York, 1905.

[39] R. T. Haslehurst, op. cit., p. 159.

3. *The Code of Canons of the African Church*, 419 A.D.

Listed in the Canons of the African Code are two interesting ones. By their wording, one seems to tolerate the theatre while stating they (dramas, etc...) should not be performed on the Lord's day, while the other Canon safeguards the moral integrity of the individual who withdrew from the actor's profession. The reader will find the text of the Canons worthy of note:

CANON LXI

Of spectacles, that they be not celebrated on Lord's days nor on the festivals of Saints.

Furthermore, it must be sought that theatrical spectacles and the exhibition of other plays be removed from the Lord's day and the other most sacred days of the Christian religion, especially because on the octave day of the holy Easter (i.e., Low Sunday) the people assemble rather at the circus than at church, and they should be transferred to some other day when they happen to fall upon a day of devotion, nor shall any Christian be compelled to witness these spectacles, especially because in the performance of things contrary to the precepts of God there should be no persecution made by anyone, but (as is right) a man should exercise the free will given him by God. Especially also should be considered the peril of the cooperators who, contrary to the precept of God, are forced by great fear to attend the shows.[40]

One would find this Canon surprisingly lacking the rigor and puritanical tone as exhibited in the writings of early African writers. Religious fervor seemed to have mellowed by this time. By stating there shall be no theatrical shows on the Lord's day or feast days, one may assume that viewing these plays on another day was tolerated.

Granted there were a variety of shows. There must have been a great desire on the part of the people to attend them, especially in large cities. When these shows fell on the same day as a religious holy day, they proved to be a hindrance to the Christian. One can easily imagine the practical implications involved. Sunday and holy days were to be days devoted to more serious affairs, benefitting one's interior life. Spectators would surely benefit,

---

[40]   Philip Schaff and Henry Wace, *Nicene and Post Nicene Fathers*, Vol. 14, p. 473, Charles Scribner's Sons, New York, 1903.

along with the working crews involved in the maintenance, arrangement of articles used on stage and the like.

Another Canon equally interesting is:

CANON LXIII

Of players who have become Christians.

And of them also it must be sought that if anyone wishes to come to the grace of Christianity from any ludicrous art (ludicra arte) and to remain free of that stain, it be not lawful for anyone to induce him or compel him to return to the performance of the same things again.

This Canon safeguards an actor's or actress' decision to refuse to return to the stage, once it was put aside for another profession.

4. *Council in Trullo*, 692 A.D.[41]

Among the many Canons concerned about various troublesome items, are several which treat the unsolved question of the theatre. It would seem that as late as this Council, there are still laws being promulgated for show goers. It is no longer a question of pagan influence as in the past; what constitutes the danger now is the use of dishonest and obscene speech. Canon XXIV informs us that even then, the newlyweds supplied their guests with live entertainment:

CANON XXIV

No one who is on the priestly catalogue nor any monk is allowed to take part in horse-races or to assist at theatrical representations. But if any clergyman be called to a marriage, as soon as the games begin let him rise up and go out. And if any one shall be convicted of such an offense let him cease therefrom or be deposed.

The following Canon makes it quite definite that no cleric may pursue a career as an actor. If he does, he is to be disposed. The outcome is not favorable for the laity either:

---

[41] Op. cit., pp. 376-394, also known as the "Quinsext" Council.

CANON LI

This holy and ecumenical synod altogether forbids those who are called "players", and their "spectacles", as well as the exhibition of hunts, and the theatrical dances. If any one despises the present canon, and gives himself to any of the things which are forbidden if he be a cleric he shall be deposed, but if a layman let him be cut off.

The next Canon seems to have left an influence especially in the West, right into the Middle Ages.

5. *Council of Elvira*, 305 A.D.

An early prohibition discouraging acting is found in Canon LXII of the Council of Elvira, Spain. This Canon states that if charioteers (aurigae) or pantomimes (pantomimi) wish to embrace the Christian faith — all well and good (placuit). If they wish to resume their former occupation, however, they are to be asked to leave the Christian community (PL 84:301).

CANON LXII

... Moreover we drive away from the life of Christians the dances given in the names of those falsely called gods by the Greeks whether of men or women, and which are performed after an ancient and un-Christian fashion; decreeing that no man from this time forth shall be dressed as a woman, nor any woman in the garb suitable to men. Nor shall he assume comic; satyric, or tragic masks....

Therefore those who in the future attempt any of these things which are written, having obtained a knowledge of them, if they be clerics we order them to be deposed, and if laymen to be cut off.

Popular Usages Creates Sense of Laxity

It is well known, that as late as the Renaissance, the transversal of sexual roles or costumes by the actor and actresses was heavily frowned upon. It is amazing to realize that of all the ecclesiastical restrictions, and popular usages, this particular Canon seems to have had a dynamic force which continued on right into the Renaissance. One remains astonished when it is realized how inestimable was the ecclesiastical influence in the Middle Ages with regard to the theatre. Another interesting Canon which seems to discourage 'theatrical' presentations of singing during liturgical ceremonies is Canon LXXV. It clearly states that those whose office is to sing in the Church are not to use melodies that are unsuitable for religious services; the singer should not force his voice nor shrill or screech the sung text.

One is led to believe that this Canon discouraged any attempt on the part of the singer to put on his 'own show'.

St. Augustine's Sermon

One gets the impression that there existed a certain amount of laxity when he reads the image St. Augustine has contained in his sermon (311)[42] for the feast of St. Cyprian. In this sermon he asks his congregation: "What is pantomiming but the harmony of the body's members set to music with gestures? ...What is our song, brothers? You heard the chanter, (perhaps a liturgical text was referred to) now, let us listen to the pantomimes, then make a harmonious (congruentia) parallel of your morals with the body movements which are performed by the pantomimes (saltatores). Within your hearts, this should take place: let evil be rooted up, only to be replaced by planting love. Only good could come from this tree.... St. Augustine continues: "Several years ago in this very place, where St. Cyprian is buried, an incident happened, which is still in the memory of our elders, — this very spot was invaded by that plague and freakishness (petulantia) of pantomiming. Throughout the night those visions (nefaria) one sang and acted with musical accompaniment (cantantibus saltabatur)". St. Augustine reassures them that he is better at being a minister of God than at being an actor. (Melius minister sum, quam actor). The whole theme is cleverly handled by referring to the Scripture quote of Matthew 11:17: "We piped you a tune but you did not dance!" This episode was not an isolated incident. The Church must have housed such performances. Still there was an air of conflict between prohibition and laxity.

---

[42] PL 38:1410, author's translation.

6. The Council of Toledo III, 589 A.D.

It is not surprising to read a similar prohibition of such activities in the Church, as stated in the Canons of the Council of Toledo III, 589 A.D. Canon XXIII states, more or less, that the profane practice which the people are accustomed to have for the solemnity of the saints should be done away with, so that the people who ought to attend the religious services be not annoyed or distracted in their devotions by the pantomimes and (their) noisy vulgar songs (saltationibus et turpibus... Canticis).[43] This state of affairs must have been widespread throughout the Iberian Church for even the various councils of Braga (610, 813, 816 A.D.) strongly condemns 'histriones' and mimes.[44] It is no wonder to learn that years later a certain fusion would have developed between religious texts and popular performances which gave rise to a sort of distorted development as we find in the *Feast of the Ass*. After reading ecclesiastical prohibitions and the secular attitude toward the theatre, one forms an opinion that although the clergy promulgated the many restrictions, the laity, on the contrary gave them very little heed, or the influence of the secular power overruled, at times. This sort of impression is readily had after reading an incident in Paul the Deacon's *History of the Lombards*.

> "When he (the emperor) was about to accept the imperial crown, and the people were expecting him at the spectacle in the circus according to usage, he first proceeded through the consecrated places, then he called to him the pontiff of the city and entered the palace with the consuls and prefects, and clad in purple, crowned with the diadem and placed upon the imperial throne he was confirmed with immense applause..."[45]

Early Medieval Witness to Popular Inclination Toward the Dramatic

1. St. Isidore, 580-836 A.D.

There Is in early medieval writings, an objective presentation of the no-

---

[43] PL 84:355, author's translation.
[44] Davidson, Charles, *Studies in the English Mystery Plays*, p. 80.
[45] *History of the Lombards,* Paul the Deacon (720-799 A.D.), Book III, Ch. XII, Translated by William D. Foulke, University of Pennsylvania Press, Philadelphia, Pennsylvania, 1974.

tion of the theatre. We find this interesting reference in the *Etymologiae* of St. Isidore of Seville. In this work, St. Isidore portrays the various components of the theatre in an almost encyclopedic style. His objective work supplied knowledge in various fields for the medieval student. With a sigh of relief, the reader will not notice the absence of prohibitions and the lack of a disciplinary tone in reference to the theatre.

St. Isidore writes, in Book XVII, Chapters 41-47[46] the origin of the word theatre in Greek, meaning 'to be in sight of' because the audience was watching the players within its reach. He adds the Latin word for it as well — PROSTIBULO, because at the end of the performances, the harlots would gather there (ibi meretrices prostabant) with the intent of selling themselves. It is also called a brothel (lupanar), the reason given is that the vileness of their bodies earned for these harlots the name wolf (LUPA). There, at the exit, they would snatch their prey — the miserable wretches (who were leaving the performances).

St. Isidore mentions the nature of tragedy, comedy; role of actors, jugglers, buffoons, mimes and dancers. He defines actors (HISTRIONES) as those men who dressed as women perform immodest gesturest moreover they falsify the truth, and present fables as facts, hence their name the mimes are those who imitate human situations. Before actual performing a story is told by the actor, then the story is portrayed in such a way by being adapted to body movements. Comedians are also mentioned and described as those who sing with words and gestures the immodest exploits of lovers.

It would appear to the reader that there is a perjorative overtone in his description of the nature of the theatre and justly so, however, it must be remembered he is writing in a Christian society and relating facts as they are. Still the overall picture one is left with is that the theatre is not a place for a Christian to frequent.

2. *Theodora*, 500-548 A.D.

This action should conclude with the irony of the empress-actress Theodora. In her, one sees the religious prohibitions unheeded, the personification of the theatre's evils all in one person what the theatre stood for, and the laxity of the Christian populace. Procopius, the private secretary and legal adviser to Belisarius, writes in his work: *The Secret History...*

---
[46] *Etimologias*, San Isidro de Sevilla; author's translation from the Spanish.

..."as soon as she (Theodora) was old enough, she joined the women on stage...she merely sold her attractions to anyone who came along. Later she joined the actors and played a regular part in their stage performances, making herself the butt of their ribald buffoonery...She was the sort of girl who if somebody walloped her or boxed her ears would make a jest of it and roar with laughter, she herself by cracking dirty jokes would invite all who came her way...often in the theatre in full view of all she would stand bare in their midst. Servants on whom this task had been imposed would sprinkle barley grains over her private parts, and geese trained for the purpose used to pick them off one by one with their bills and swallow them...She encouraged shamelessness... parading her own special kind of gymnastics...As for her fellow actresses, she habitually and constantly stormed at them like a fury; for she was malicious in the extreme."[47]

A point of interest is to mention the fact that Theodora later became involved in rehabilitating prostitutes by founding a convent for them. Ironically enough, a vivid mosaic of her is preserved in the Church of San Vitale, Ravenna.[48]

The fact that the Church had made itself the focal point of communal activities led to the eventual introduction within its walls of the dramatic impulses of the faithful, which as we have seen, contained subjects irreverent or indecent, unworthy to be presented in such a hallow place. It is quite evident that there was a certain type of dramatic activity alive among the people. From the days of Terullian, who viewed the rejection of the theatre as a sign of one's allegiance to Christ, to Theodora, who although an actress, involved herself in Church-state affairs, an underlining and deep rooted desire to perform was manifested and somehow associated with religious and liturgical texts. We have but to admit that some type of dramatic activity was going on. These liturgical texts were the source of this dramatic outlet, and it was surely on the rise throughout the Empire, in spite of the Council prohibitions. From the liturgical texts, the Church was indirectly fostering a dramatic reenactment of the people's faith. We will find it supporting now to investigate the various texts and discover how this was accomplished.

---

[47] *The Secret history*, Procopius, Penguin Books, pp. 83-85.
[48] *New Catholic Encyclopedia*, Vol. XIV, p. 15. The nineteenth century French playwright, Victorien Sardou (1831-1908) who wrote the libretto for *Tosca* also wrote a play based on the life of Theodora (1884). Later J. Massenet wrote music for an opera with the same name, with Sara Bernhardt in the leading role.

III
Notion of Worship —
From Text to Performance

It would be almost inconceivable to think of any religious form of worship without a primary text or written material of some definite kind on which to rely on for ritual or to serve as a formulation of belief. An author[49] expresses this idea very clearly when she writes that worship first appears as a spontaneous reaction to encounter the divine, then develops into something which must be done. It is not surprising to find the concrete expression of worship in ritual acts in every society; it is through these ritual acts that man can do these things together. This ritual combines agreed speech, gestures, and additional ceremonies into one expression of worship. By this combination, man is likewise united by his physical, mental and emotional responses in evoking a religious attitude with the desire for a repeated performance for the benefit of all taking part.

1. *Evidence In Ancient World — Pagan*

Similar ideas are expressed by another author; speaking of seasonal myths, he says:

> "In the former case, the durative significance of the ritual is simply taken for granted... that the performers are at the same time acting out

---

[49]   Evelyn Underhill, *Worship*, pp. 13, 23, 33.

an ideal situation and endued with an ideal, preterpuncutal character. This we may suppose to have been the primitive stage, and hence the earliest form of drama...ritual then becomes subsumed in myth. The participants are no longer protagonists of a direct experience but mere actors (personae). ..dramatic ritual then become drama proper."[50]

2. Evidence in Ancient World — Biblical

A. 2 Chron. 29:22-28

For our purposess we will mention the use of ritual in the Judeo-Christian tradition. An elaborate liturgy with striking ritualistic overtones can be read in 2 Chron. 29:22-28. The rite based on the text was very similar to the pagan sacrifical rite, and this had to be so, for if the magnificent ceremonial rites of the surrounding pagans were not to have a deep influence on the Hebrew people, then some external concessions had to be made lest idol worship be more sensuous, pleasing and attractive.

> "They slaughtered the bulls, and the priests collected the blood and cast it on the altar. Then they slaughtered the rams and cast the blood on the altar; then they slaughtered the lambs and cast the blood on the altar. Then the he-goats for the sin offering were led before the king and the assembly, who had laid their hands upon them. The priests then slaughtered them and offered their blood on the altar to atone for the sin of all Israel; for "The holocaust and the sin offerings," the king had said, "is for all Israel."
> He stationed the Levites in the Lord's house with cymbals, harps and lyres according to the prescriptions of David, of Cad the king's seer, and of Nathan the prophet; for the prescriptions were from the Lord through his prophets. The Levites were stationed with the instruments of David, and the priests with the trumpets. Then Hezekiah ordered the holocaust to be sacrificed on the altar, and in the same instant that the holocaust began, they also began the song to the Lord, to the accompaniment of the trumpets and the instruments of David, king of Israel. The entire assembly prostrated itself, and they continued to

---

50 Theodor H. Caster, *Thespis*, pp. 79-83. See also the Extract, *Ritual Ceremonies* — 1931 by Lucien Levy Bruhl.

sing the song and to sound the trumpets until the holocaust had been completed. As the holocaust was completed, the king and all who were with him knelt and prostrated themselves."

B.   Psalms

The Psalms, religious songs of praise, laments, hymns for liturgical functions, have the invitation to a specific form of external prayer composed within the very Psalm itself. It is a clear example of the union of blending of both text and performance. Worthy of note are:

Ps. 33: 3   Give thanks to the Lord on the harp, with the ten-stringed lyre chant his praises.
         3   Sing to him a new song;
             Pluck the strings skillfully, with shouts of gladness

Ps. 47: 2   All you peoples, clap your hands
             shout to God with cries of gladness...
         7   Sing praise to our God, sing praise...

Ps. 81:   Liturgical directives clearly seen here:
         2   Sing joyfully to God our strength...
         3   Take up a melody, and sound the timbrel...
         4   Blow the trumpet at the new moon...

Ps. 95: 1   Come, let us sing joyfully to the Lord:
         2   Let us greet him with thanksgiving...
         6   Come, let us bow down in worship,
             Let us kneel before the Lord who made us.

Ps.100   A Psalm of Thanksgiving
         1   Sing joyfully to the Lord, all you lands;
         2   Come before him with joyful song
         4   Enter his gates with thanksgiving,
             his courts with praise.

Ps.134		Exortation to the night watch to Bless the Lord
	1	Come bless the Lord...
		Who stand in the house of the Lord.
	2	Lift up your hands toward the sanctuary,
		and bless the Lord.

Ps. 24		The Lord's solemn entry into Zion
	7	Lift up, O gates, your lintels;
		reach up, you ancient portals,
		that the king of glory may come in!
	8	Who is the king of glory?
		The Lord, strong and mighty,
		the Lord, mighty in battle.
	9	Lift up, O gates, your lintels...,
	10	Who is this king of Glory?
		The Lord of hosts; he is the
		king of glory

3. Evidence from the New Testament

A. The Lord's Supper

It would be helpful, at this point, to emphasize and clarify the whole aspect of Christian ritual, worship and performance before one ventures toward the dramatization of the religious texts.

Ritual indeed has a fundamental link with mystery, for as Odo Casel defines mystery, this notion becomes apparent:

"The mystery is a sacred ritual action in which a saving deed is made present through the rite; the congregation by performing the rite, take part in the saving act, and thereby win salvation".[51]

There is a similar expression in the work of A. Dukes which seems to parallel this idea:

---

[51] Casel, *The Mystery of Christian Worship*, p. 54.

"...the audience of drama sprang from the rank of the performers."[52]

This saving act for the faithful is God's design to save. The passion, death and resurrection of Jesus, the Lord, is the mystery of redemption, the peak of God's plan. Through His death, the Lord leads the way to salvation and endless joy. For this reason the Lord instituted the great mystery of His love as the last act of His life on earth: on the night before He died, He gave to His disciples this mystical celebration of His redeeming deed. So then, that sacred rite is what the disciples are to act in memory; they are to make real the sufferings, death and resurrection of the Lord of ages. Christ gave this gift to His Church's care who acts it out and fulfills His request 'do this in remembrance of me'. This saving act continues in the sacraments, especially in the Eucharist; around which all the other sacraments revolve. This is the mystery of faith, and faith alone can grasp the inner reality.

4. Evidence from the Christian Community

A. *St. Thomas Aquinas*, 1224-1274 A.D.

St. Thomas Aquinas treats this aspect of faith, in his *Pange Lingua*, with the idea of letting faith supply that which is lacking to the human senses. The sacred rites help the senses perceive the invisible inner, though real entity. Now the question may arise: 'How does the mystery of Christ differ from the mystery of worship?'

B. Vatican Council II. 1982-1965 A.D.

The mind of the Church is clearly expressed with the words of the Constitution on the Sacred Liturgy of the Second Vatican Council:

> "The liturgy then, is rightly seen as an exercise of the priestly office of Jesus Christ. It involves the presentation of man's sanctification under the guise of signs perceptible by the senses and its accomplishment in ways appropriate to each of these signs. In it full public worship is performed by the Mystical Body of Jesus Christ, this is, by the

---

[52] Dukes, *Drama*, p. 26.

ship is performed by the Mystical Body of Jesus Christ, this is, by the Head and his members.... The Church performs together with him the role of priest and victim, offers him to the Father and at the same time makes a total offering of herself together with him...Consequently the more intelligible the signs by which it is celebrated and worshipped, the more firmly and effectively, it will enter into the minds and lives of the faithful.

It is not surprising at all that the Eastern Orthodox view is similar in essence:

"It is not merely a commemoration of the events of the Gospel or other events in Christ's life, in an artistic form.... The Christmas service does not merely commemorate the birth of Christ. In it Christ is truly born in a mystery, as at Easter He rises again. The life of the Church in her liturgy, discloses to our senses the continuing mystery of the Incarnation. The Lord still lives in the Church...and it is the function of that Church to make those sacred memories living...so that we take part in them."[53]

One wonders what the reaction of St. Clement of Alexandria would have been if he were to know that centuries later, someone would write:

"....The initiate may either be a mere witness of the divine drama or take part in it...or he may see himself identified through the ritual action with the god....This participation in the ritual event gives rise, among other effects, to that hope of immortality which is characteristic of the Eleusinian mysteries. A living example of the mystery drama representing the permanence as well as the transformation of life is the Mass...during this sacred rite we note all degrees of participation, from mere indifferent attendance to the profoundest emotion. The groups ...despite their inattention, participate in the sacred action by their mere presence in this place where grace abounds. The Mass is an extramundane and extratemporal act in which Christ is sacrificed...and this rite of his sacrificial death is not a repetition of the historical event but the original, unique, and eternal act. The experience of the Mass is

---

[53]Underhill, *Worship*, p. 76, quoting S. Bougahoff's *L'Orthodixie*, p. 180.

therefore a participation in the transcendence of life...it is a moment of eternity in time."[54]

St. Thomas Aquinas is well known for his synthesis of Aristotelian philosophy and Christian thought, as well as the fact that he composed liturgical texts for the then newly proclaimed feast of Corpus Christi, by Pope Urban IV in 1264. One recalls that during that century, the stage of European drama was well on its way as being a polished art form.

---

[54]   Jung, *Four Archetypes*, Essay II Concerning Rebirth, p. 51-52.

IV
The Nature of Worship Itself Entails the Sense of the Dramatic

Many questions were posed, no doubt, dealing with the church's ceremonies that tended to portray theatrical elements. In his *Summa Theologica*, (Part I of Second Part. Q. 101 Art. 2,3; Q. 102 Art. 4) St. Thomas affirms that Divine worship is internal and external. Since man is composed of body and soul, each of these should be applied to the worship of God, the body by an outward worship, the soul by an interior worship. But then when arranged in liturgical celebrations, they tend to be theatrical. Now, to the objection that such performance savor of the theatre i.e. actions done to represent the actions of others, St. Thomas replies by stating that human reason fails to grasp certain expressions so there is a need of signs by means of sensible figures to grasp the sublimity of the truth contained in these celebrations. Moreover, special vessels and special ministers had to be selected for worship so that the soul of man might be brought to greater reverence for God.

Ever faithful to the command of its Founder,[55] the Church celebrated the Lord's Supper throughout the ages. Inevitably, the natural tendency of the believers' spirit was to contribute much external decoration to accompany the last wishes of the Lord. Soon the simple meal atmosphere was enriched with ritual and signs which symbolized the reality of Christ's presence and His saving power at the present, while it afforded the believer the opportunity to give glory to God. By Baptism, one is made a member of Christ's body,

---

[55]   1 Cor. 11:26, 'Do this in memory of me'.

hence the duty to take part in the Eucharist is established, by this, one finds that a sharing in divine activity is made possible, and so it is — the actions must be spiritualized by the words, otherwise the whole ritual may degenerate into magic or mere superstition. From the earliest accounts which describe the Church's enactment of the Eucharist, one is aware that that very act has always been intimately associated with the words that are considered sacred. The following observations will afford us some examples of the tendency of the Church to combine and foster its sacred text with an external bodily accompaniment. Among the many liturgical texts of antiquity, the selected following will serve our purpose and interest.

Evidence of Dramatic Impulse in Early Liturgical Texts

1. *Pre-Nicene Period*
   A. *Didache* — the so-called Teachings of the Twelve Apostles

($\Delta\iota\delta\alpha\chi\eta$ $\tau\omega\nu$ $\delta\omega\delta\epsilon\kappa\alpha$ $\alpha\pi\sigma\sigma\tau\sigma\lambda\sigma\nu$) -didache meaning teaching, hence its title. It was written around 90 A.D., as a guide book with instructions for the laity.

Chapter IX treats the notion of Eucharist as public prayer.

The Thanksgiving (Eucharist)

Now concerning the Thanksgiving (Eucharist), ($\epsilon\mu\chi\alpha\rho\iota\sigma\tau\iota\alpha s$) thus give thanks ($\epsilon\mu\chi\alpha\rho\iota\sigma\rho\eta$. $\sigma\alpha\rho\epsilon$) thus first, for the cup: We thank you, O Our Father for the holy vine of David...

Then for the broken bread:

We thank you, O Our Father for life and knowledge...

Chapter X ..After you are filled, give thanks thus: We thank O holy Father for your holy name which you enshrined in our hearts...let the prophets give thanks as much as they will:

Chapter XIV..Come together on the Lord's own day ($\varkappa\alpha\tau\rho\alpha$ $\varkappa\upsilon\rho\iota\alpha\varkappa\eta\nu$ $\delta\eta$ $\varkappa\upsilon\rho\iota\sigma\nu$) break bread and give thanks, having first confessed your sins that your sacrifice may be pure. He who has a dispute with his neighbor must not join with you before he has been reconciled....

Included in the directives is the possible allowance for the prophets to improvise. Without discussing the theological overtones and possibility as to whether this text depicts a home celebration of the Eucharist, one thing remains clear — the presence of a loose ritual and text. It was only much later when rites would become more and more imposing, complicated and fixed. Until that point was reached, the individual improvisation of the celebrant remained rather fluid.

One would naturally wonder what the Eucharistic celebration was like in the second century.

B. *St. Justin, Martyr*

In his *First Apology* c. 150, Justin presents the outline of the Eucharist as celebrated in Rome. It is the oldest piece of evidence we have concerning the assembly and worship of the early Christians. His interesting presentation lacking text of prayer, makes it possible for us to view the celebrating assembly at that early stage in Christian history. He says:

> "On the day which is called the day of the sun we have a common assembly...the memoirs of the Apostles or the writings of the Prophets are read as long as there is time...when the reader has finished, the president of the assembly verbally admonishes...then we all stand and offer up our prayers... At the conclusion of the prayers we greet one another with a kiss... bread and wine are presented. He who presides offers up prayers and thanksgivings to the beast of his ability saying —Amen. The Eucharistic elements are distributed and consumed by those present"...[56]

The reader would get the impression that the president (of the assembly) offered prayers as best he could, that is, the prayers were improvised compositions. We will see that as late as 215 A.D. Hippolytus advises that bishops should pray according to their individual ability. This observation

---

[56] John Miller C.S.C., *Fundamentals of the Liturgy* (Notre Dame, Indiana 1959), p. 45.

would indicate that a text, even extemporaneously uttered, fostered a dramatic attitude on the part of the worshippers.

   C.   Apostolic Tradition of Hippolytus of Rome, written c. 215 A.D. also known by the name *Canon of Hippolytus*.

This work is the oldest text of a Mass formulary that has come down to us. What makes the whole thing interesting is the fact that Justin gave the impression that no official texts were then in existence. Yet in Hippolytus we read after the various rules for ordinations:

> "And the bishop shall give thanks according to the aforesaid models. It is not altogether necessary for him to recite the very same words which we gave before... let each one pray according to his own ability. If he is able to pray suitably with a grand and elevated prayer, this is a good thing. But if on the other hand he should pray and recite a prayer according to a fixed form, no one shall prevent him. Only let his prayer be correct and right in doctrine.[57]

Comparing both testimonies we can conclude that Hippolytus suggests fixed formulas which are to be considered as samples or models. Words could be composed by the celebrant himself provided he remain true to the established intention of the Church. The overall impression one gets is that texts are not really fixed, nonetheless the words of prayer uttered "extempore" by the celebrant afforded enough basis for an externalized ritual. We will consider interesting points of the text itself.

After the Preface is prayed, the directive is given to introduce the Canon or Eucharistic Prayer — and he continues thus:

'We render thanks to you, O God,...'

This structure thanks the Father for Creation and the Incarnation, then there are the words of institution, verbal command of Jesus to repeat this action in His memory (Anamnesis), calling down the Holy Spirit to effect the presence and unity of Jesus Christ (Epiclesis). The doxology put a neat finishing touch

---

[57]   Josef A. Jungmann, S.J. *The Early Liturgy*, (Notre Dame, Indiana 1959), p. 65.

to the canon, which is orderly and clear in expressing a belief throughout its rather short version. Although there are directives within the canon itself, one must consider the entire canon as a directive for the celebrant. The dialogue and directives continue:

> And the bishop shall say: "And again we ask you Almighty God, etc.
>
> The deacon shall say: "bow down your heads."
>
> The bishop shall say: "Look down, bless both men and women..."
>
> And the deacon shall say: "Let us attend".
>
> And the bishop shall say: "Holiness to holy ones".
>
> And the people shall say: "...Amen"
>
> And the bishop shall say: "The Lord be with you".
>
> And the people shall say: "And with your spirit"
>
> And the deacon shall say: "Go in peace."[58]

In canon 37 of Hippolytus' work we read that when a bishop celebrates the Eucharist the presbyters who stand by him should be clothed in white.

2. Post Nicene Period

A. The Apostolic Constitutions C.A.D. 375

This compilation, most likely Syrian in origin, was brought to completion at the end of the fourth century. The sections that will be of interest for our observation are found in Book II, 57 and Book VIII, 5-15. It would be quite evident that the celebration of the Eucharist became more developed, organized and expanded. We will discuss these selections respectively. The

---

[58] Josef A. Jungmann, S.J. *The Early Liturgy*, pp. 529-520 Latin version; for English translation, cf. Gregory Dix, *The Shape of the Liturgy*, pp. 157-158.

bishop is exhorted to appoint deacons as mariners to prepare places for the faithful as passengers on a ship, under the commander of the assembly —the bishop. These sound a bit like stage direction and preparation for the coming performane.

a)   Book II, Chapter 57:

"...In the middle let the bishop's throne be place on each side of him let the presbytery sit down; and let the deacons stand near at hand, in close and small girt garments, for they are like mariners and managers of the ship: with regard to these, let the laity sit on the other side, with all quietness and good order. And let the women sit by themselves, they also keeping silence. In the middle, let the reader stand upon some high place."

This selection would indicate that certain types of vestments were worn for the celebration. Not only are they in white, as we read a while ago, but also their size and fit is, by now, a fixed feature. One cannot help associate this fact with the costume design of a certain play character which the audience expects.

The document continues:

"And while the Gospel is read, let all the presbyters and deacons, and all the people, stand up in great silence...

In the next place, lat the presbyters one by one, not all together, exhort the people, and the bishop in the last place, as being the commander. Let the porters stand at the entries of the men, and observe them...

But if any one be found sitting out of his place, let him be rebuked by the deacon, as a manager of the foreship..."

But if any one be found sitting out of his place, let him be rebuked by the deacon, as a manager of the foreship..."

Let the young persons sit by themselves, if there be a place for them; if not, let them stand upright. But let those that are already stricken in years sit in order. For the children which stand, let their fathers and mothers take them to them. Let the younger women also sit by themselves, if there be a place for them; but if there be not, let them stand behind the women. Let those women which are married and have children, be placed by themselves; but let the virgins, and the widows, and the elder woinen, stand or sit before all the rest; and let the deacon be the disposer of the places, that every one of those that comes in may go to his proper place, and may not sit at the entrance. In like manner, let the deacon oversee the people, that nobody may whisper, nor slumber, nor laugh, nor nod; for all ought in the church to stand wisely, and soberly, and attentively, having their attention f-ixed upon the word of the Lord..."

In setting the mood and atmosphere for a proper dignified celebration, the role of deacon seems to have been very much like the role of a theatre usher, to prepare the audience and help set the mood before the actual performance begins.

"...After this let all rise up with one consent, and looking towards the east....

As to the deacons, after the prayer is over, let some of them attend upon the oblation of the Eucharist, ministering to the Lord's body with fear. Let others of them watch the multitude, and keep them silent. But let that deacon who is at the priest's hand say to the people, Let no one have any quarrel against another...

After this let the deacon pray for the whole church, for the whole world...

This selection indicates the important role played by the deacon — the liaison between audience (faithful) and major character (the officiating bishop).

The instruction continues...

After this let the priest pray for peace upon the people and bless them, as Moses commanded: "The Lord bless thee, and keep thee: the Lord make His face to shine upon thee, "and give thee peace."[59] Let the bishop pray for the people, and say: Save Thy people, O Lord, and bless Thine inheritance...After this let the sacrifice follow, the people standing, and praying silently; and when the oblation has been

---

[59]   Num. V 1:24 etc...

47

made, let every rank by itself partake of the Lord's body and precious blood in order, and approach with reverence and holy fear, as to the body of their king...let the door be watched, lest any unbeliever, or one not yet initiated, come in.

One notices the directives set for the celebrants, accompanied with Scriptural texts the contexts of their prayer together with body postures. A plea for courtesy is noted in the manner of approaching the actual reception of Communion. It would seem the whole body of the faithful "acted" as a whole in one designated place excluding the unprepared i.e., those not baptised as yet. It is quite evident that an interrelationship between text of the liturgy and gesture became noticeable and more intensified both for the priests and laity in public worship.

b) *Book VIII Chapters 4-15*

The following selections will undoubtedly show the external mood and manner linked to a liturgical formula. Here we read of an episcopal ordination; a glimpse of one of the earliest descriptions of that rite is presented:

> ... And silence being made, let one of the principal bishops, together with two others, stand near to the altar, the rest of the bishops and presbyters praying silently, and the deacons holding the divine Gospels open upon the head of him that is to be ordained, and say to God thus:.....

a lengthy prayer then follows.[60]
    We read on:

> ... And after the prayer let one of the bishops elevate the sacrifice upon the hands of him that is ordained, and early in the morning let him be placed in his throne, in a place set apart for him among the rest of the bishops, they all giving him the kiss of the Lord. And after the reading of the Law and the Prophets, and our Epistles, and Acts, and the Gospels, let him that is ordained salute the Church, saying:

---

[60]   *Apostolic Constitution*, Book VIII, Chapter 4.

The grace of our Lord Jesus Christ, the love of God and the Father, and the fellowship of the Holy Ghost, be with you all:

and let them all answer: And with Thy Spirit.

And after these words let him speak to the people the words of exhortation; and when he has ended his word, all standing up let the deacon ascend upon some high seat, and proclaim: Let none of the hearers, let none of the unbelievers stay; and silence being made, let him say: You Catechumens pray:

And let the deacon bid prayers for them saying: 'Let us all pray to God for the Catechumens...'

The deacon continues with exhortations as: "Let us still earnestly lift up our supplications for them.... Then again: "Rise up, you Catechumens, beg for yourselves the peace of God...bow down your heads and receive the blessing. At the naming of every one by the deacon, as we said before, let the people say: Lord have mercy on him, let the children say it first. And as they have bowed down their heads, let the bishop bless them with the blessing:

'O God Almighty...look upon your servants, give them a new heart ...make them partakers of your divine mysteries...Amen.'

And after this let the deacon say: "Go out you Catechumens, in peace!' A similar rite is performed for those tormented by the devil, and for those preparing their final tasks for the deception of baptism. The format is the same for the penitents. We see that the deacon, the bridge between clergy and laity, invites the congregation to pray for the various persons who as yet should not assist at the Mysteries. The deacon gives an outline of his prayer by mentioning the intentions and the things to be prayed for. The faithful answer, especially the children, by praying "Lord have mercy'. When the Catechumens se up, the deacon again bids them to join with him in prayer. He bids them to bow for the bishop's blessing; after this the deacon sends them out. After a long litany prayed by the deacon and those fully initiated into the Mysteries, the bishop concludes with a solemn prayer of confidence. The deacon continues:

"Let us attend".

The bishop greets the people by saying:

"The peace of God be with you all."

The people answer:

"And also with you."

The deacon says to all:

"Greet each other with the holy kiss (kiss of peace)."

The document continues to give instructions:

> And let the clergy salute the bishop, the men of the laity salute the men, the women the women. And let the children stand at the reading-desk (pulpit for scripture reading) and let the deacon stand by them, that they may not be disorderly. And let other deacons walk about and watch the men and women, that no tumult may be made, and that no one nod, or whisper, or slumber and let the deacons stand at the doors of the men, and the sub-deacons at those of the women, that no one go out, nor a door be opened, although it be for one of the faithful, at the time of the oblation. But let one of the sub-deacons b-ring water to wash the hands of the priests, which is a symbol of the purity of those souls that are devoted to God.

Chapter XII continues with the instructions that "the deacon shall immediately say:

> 'Let none of the Catechumens...
> Let none of the unbelievers stay here.'

The text continues:

> "When this is done, let the deacons bring the gifts to the bishop at the altar, and let the presbyters stand on his right hand and on his left, as the presbyters stand before their Master.[61] Let two of the deacons,

---

[61] It is worthwhile mentioning the fact that symbolism is mentioned here — so

on each side of the altar, hold a fan, made up of thin membranes, or of feathers of the peacock, or of fine cloth, and let them silently drive away the small animals that fly about, that they may not come near to the cups (chalices)'. Surely the attractive colors of the fan, must have added some theatrical setting, even if the fan was used for the practical purpose of chasing flies away from the wine filled chalices, which after the consecration in the Liturgy would be the true presence of Christ, later to be consumed by the faithful in Holy Communion.

The directives continue:

'Let the priest...put on his shining garment, and stand at the altar, and make the sign of the cross upon his forehead with his hand and say:
'The grace of almighty God...be with you all.'
And let all with one voice say:
'And with thy spirit.'
The priest says:
'Lift up your mind.'
All the people:
'We lift it up unto the Lord.'
All the people:
'It is meet and right to do.'
Then let the priest say: 'It is right to sing a hymn to Thee, who art true God...'
And let all the people say: Holy, holy, holy Lord of hosts, heaven and earth are full of His glory.'

Afterwards let the priest say:

For Thou are truly holy...

...Being mindful, therefore of those things that He endured for our sakes, we give Thee thanks, O God Almighty, not in such a manner as we ought, but as we are able, and fulfill His constitution: "For in the same night that He was betrayed, He took bread" in His holy and

---

early in church history. We will see how it is later used by church writers in their commentaries on the Liturgy.

undefiled hands, and, looking up to Thee His God and Father, "He brake it, and gave it to His disciples, saying, This is the mystery of the new covenant: take of it and eat. This is my body, which is broken for many, for the remission of sins."

Finally the priest finishes the lengthy eucharistic prayer and all the people answer: Amen, to the doxology. This ratifies their own participation in the celebration. The deacon then calls the faithful's attention to the celebrant's invitation:

'Holy things for holy people',

to which the people answer:

'There is one only holy one, one only Lord Jesus...to the glory of the Father. Amen.[62]

The celebrant receives Communion, then the other priests and deacons then all the people in order, with reverence and calm. The directive for the celebrant in distributing the Eucharist to the faithful is:

"The Body of Christ' while the recipient replies: 'Amen'.

When the deacon gives the chalice he is to say:

'The Blood of Christ, the cup of life', here too the recipient answers: 'Amen'.

While the faithful are approaching the area to receive, they are accompanied with Psalm 33, in which the words: 'Taste and see how gracious is the Lord' have a fitting place in the ceremony. Even the text of this Psalm adds to their performance, in this case, approaching the Sanctuary.

When all have received the Eucharist in Holy Communion, the deacon again invites the faithful to thank God for receiving and dedicate themselves to God. After being asked by the deacon to bow for

---

[62] Later on we will see how this section of the ceremony developed into a more elaborate form of blessing.

the blessing of the ce1lebrant they depart at the words of the deacon's dismissal: 'Go in peace'.

C. *St. Ambrose 339-397 A.D.*

While bishop of Milan, St. Ambrose wrote his work *De Sacramentis*, which consisted of homilies directed to the newly baptized. The rhetorical style he uses incites in their minds the memory of their own baptism which took place that previous Saturday evening — the Paschal Vigil. It is by the use of this very style that we get a glimpse of the baptismal ceremony as performed at Milan in that specific time.

It is precisely the personal approach with which St. Ambrose writes, that we find the text interesting as well as informative. One observe in *De Sacamentis II, V*:

> "Now, then, let us take thought. A priest comes; he says a prayer at the font, he uses heavenly words.. because they are Christ's."

Chapter VI:

> "Now let us examine what it is that is called baptism! You came to the font, you went down into it; you gave heed to the priest; you saw the deacons and the priest at the font....Then earth does not wash, but water washes. Therefore, the font is as a sepulture."

Chapter VII:

> "So you dipped; you came to the priest. What did he say to you? He said: 'God...who regenerated you by water and the Holy Spirit...will anoint you unto life everlasting."

Chapter III, I

> "You came up from the font. What followed? You heard the reading. The girded priest...washed your feet. What mystery is this?...We are aware of the fact that the Church in Rome does not have this custom, whose character and form we follow in all things. Yet it does not have the custom of washing the feet. So note: perhaps on account of the

multitude this practice is declined...therefore, you wash the feet that you may wash away the poison of the serpent."

Chapter II

"After this what follows? You are able to come to the altar. Since you have come, you are able to see what you did not see before."

Chapter IV, II

"There follows your coming to the altar...You come then, desiring. You come to the altar desiring to receive the sacrament. Your soul says: 'And I will go to the altar of God' (Ps. 42:4)."

Chapter V

"Look at these events one by one. It says: 'On the day before He ouffered, He took bread...Before it is consecrated, it is bread: but when Christ's words have been added, it is the body of Christ.

...So you say not indifferently 'Amen', confessing in spirit that you receive the body of Christ. Therefore, when...the priest says to you: 'The Body of Christ,' you say: 'Amen' what the tongue confesses let the affection hold.'

Chapter III

'...You have come, then, to the altar, you have received the grace of God...the church rejoices that the members of her household are at hand dressed in white. You have this in the Canticle of Canticles...: Let my beloved come into His garden and eat the fruits of His apple trees (Cant. 5:1).' What are these apple trees? You were made dry wood in Adam, but now through the grace of Christ you flower as apple trees.'

There are several interesting points of observation in this tractate. Beside the pleasant conversation tone of his work, St. Ambrose gives us the information to conclude for ourselves that the ceremonies at the Easter Vigil were so elaborate that they would surely Impress the memories of the new Christians throughout their lives. Their being vested with a white garment, which was to be worn throughout the week of Easter, must have been very impressive. The mentioning of the washing of the feet during the baptismal ceremony is very interesting, for it informs us of a usage foreign to Rome but quite common in Southern Gaul. These local variations in the liturgy will become more fixed and more pronounced as the years go by. The washing of the neophytes' feet took place with the words similar to these spoken by the celebrant:

> 'I wash your feet, as Our Lord, Jesus Christ, did to His disciples so that you would do the same to foreigners and travelers for life eternal.'[63]

St. Ambrose also uses symbolism; this will also become more elaborate with many writers in the Church, as time goes on. One would not find it exceptional that these liturgical actions were always initiated or accompanied by the texts from the Scriptures.

D. *St. Cyril of Jerusalem* c. 313-386 A.D.

It was an established custom to baptize the Catechumens at Easter. They also received Confirmation and the Holy Eucharist at that one ceremony. Like St. Ambrose in Milan, St. Cyril delivers his lectures to the newly initiated, to help them learn more of the mysteries they are involved in, hence the name — *Catecheses Mystagogicae*. From the literary point of view, one notices that both works constitute a new literary genre. These lectures, delivered in the Church of the Resurrection (Anastasis) built over the Holy Sepulchre in Jerusalem, give us a very sober explanation of the symbolism underlying the religious rites. The following selections will contain material suitable for our observation.[64]

a) *Lecture I*

"...First you entered the antechamber of the baptistery and faced towards the West. On the command to stretch out your hand, you re-

---

[63] *Christian Workshop*, Msgr. L. Duchesne, p. 326, author's translation.
[64] Leo P. McCauley, S. J. and Anthony Stephenson, *The Works of St. Cyril of Jerusalem*, Catholic University of America Press, Washington, D.C.

nounced Satan as though he were there in person...You are told, however, to address him as personally present, and with arm outstretched to say: 'I renounce you, Satan. Allow me to explain the reason of your facing West, for you should know it. Because the West is the region of visible darkness, Satan, who is himself darkness, has his empire in darkness — that is the significance of renounce that gloomy Prince of night. What was it that each of you said, standing there? 'I renounce you, Satan, you wicked and cruel tyrant...Renounce, then, the works of Satan, that is, every irrational deed and thought.. Next you say, 'and all his pomp'. The pomp of the Devil is the craze for the theatre ($\theta\epsilon\alpha\tau\rho o\upsilon\mu\alpha\nu\iota\alpha\iota$), the horse races in the circus,...avoid an addiction to the theatre, with its spectacle of the licentiousness, and lewd and unseemly antics of actors and the frantic (raving) dancing ($o\rho\chi\eta\sigma\epsilon\iota s$) —could also mean pantomimic dance) of degenerates...When you renounce Satan, trampling underfoot every covenant with him... God's paradise opens before you... Symbolic of this is your facing about from the West to the East, the place of light... that was what was done in the outer chamber. When we enter... we shall receive the key to the rites performed there...\"[65]

One notices the assembly in the antechamber, and the neophytes facing westward until they renounce Satan and turn eastward. The words accompanied by their body gestures would render their profession of faith more emphatic. The religious processions conducted by the pagans were known as 'pomps' (pompae), and must have been inviting as well as spectacular. For the Christian such an exhibition was contrary to the Christian way of life. Needless to mention is the obvious exhortation to shun the theatre. As much as St. Cyril was condemning the spectacular presentation at the theatre, so also was the liturgy encouraging some dramatic expression of faith on the part of the believers.

b) *Lecture II*

"...I shall, resuming from yesterday, expound the bare essentials of our next topic, explaining the symbolical meaning of what you did in the inner chamber. Immediately then, upon entering you removed your tunics. This was a figure of the 'stripping off of the old man with

---

[65]   Op. cit., pp. 153-159.

his deeds. I do not, of course, refer to this visible garment, but to the old man which is sinking towards death.... then, when stripped, you were anointed with exorcised olive oil from the topmost hairs of your head to the soles of your feet, and became partakers of the good olive tree, Jesus Christ.... After this you were conducted to the sacred pool of divine Baptism...you were asked, one by one, whether you believed in the name of the Father, etc....In the same moment you were dying and being born, and that saving water was at once your grave and your mother."

The actual baptism must have been very impressive. By entering into a pool type structure, the neophyte enacted the 'descending' into the tomb of the old life and 'rising' to new life in Christ. It was at that point of ascending from the pool, that the white tunic would be put on the new Christian, as a sign of this new dignity. After a full week of wearing this new garment, as a sign of the entry into new life, the garment was then put aside. Our own English — Low Sunday, the Sunday after Easter carries this idea to a point. The senses played an important role throughout the rite. The first anointing with oil served as a preparatory step toward Baptism; it too had some symbolic meaning.

    c) *Lecture III*

"...Beware of supposing that this ointment is mere ointment...your forehead and sense organs are sacramentally anointed, in such wise that while your body is anointed with the visible oil, your soul is sanctified by the holy, quickening Spirit. You are anointed first upon the forehead to rid you of the shame which the first human transgressor bore...then upon the ears, to receive ears quick to hear the divine mysteries. Once privileged to receive the holy Chrism you are called Christians and have a name that bespeaks your new birth..."

This anointing impressed the Christian, for the gesture suggested the Spirit's presence, and the fragrance of the oil was detected by the sense of smell. It was as though the whole individual was acted upon so as to allow the individual Christian to act forward. And this did happen. All seemed prepared and directed for the climactic peak in the initiation ceremony. In his fifth lecture, St. Cyril gives a commentary of the liturgy of which they have a part: 'to crown the work of your spiritual edification'.

d) *Lecture V*

"...You saw the deacon who offers the water for the washing of hands to the celebrant...the hands symbolize action, so by washing them we signify evidently the purity and blamelessness of our conduct...the handwashing, then, is a symbol of innocence. Next the deacon cries: 'Welcome one another', and 'Let us kiss one another'. This kiss is a sign of a true union of hearts, the kiss is a reconciliation. Then the celebrant cries: 'Lift up your hearts'...assenting your answer, 'We have lifted them up to the Lord, let no one present be so disposed that while his lips form the words, in his mind his attention is engaged by worldly thought...then the priest says: 'Let us give thanks to the Lord'...Then you say 'It is meet and just'. Next, after sanctifying ourselves by these spiritual songs, we implore the merciful God to send forth His Holy Spirit upon the offering to make the bread the Body of Christ and the wine the Blood of Christ. Next, when the spiritual sacrifice...has been completed...we beseech God...then we commemorate also those who have fallen asleep...next we pray for the Fathers and Bishops who have fallen asleep....Then, after this, we recite that prayer which the Savior delivered to His own disciples (The Lord's Prayer)....Then after completing the prayer, you say 'Amen' which means 'So be it', thus setting your seal upon the petitions....Next the priest says: 'Holy things to the holy' (**ta atia tois agios**) you say: 'One is holy, one is the Lord, Jesus Christ....After this you hear the chanter inviting you with a sacred melody to communion in the holy mysteries, in the words: O hear the chanter inviting you with a sacred melody to communion in the holy mysteries, in the words: 'O taste and see that the Lord is good'....coming up to receive, do not approach with your wrists extended..., but making your left hand a throne for the right (for it is about to receive a King) and cupping your palm, so receive the Body of Christ, and answer: 'Amen'...after partaking of the Body of Christ, approach also the chalice of His Blood. Do not stretch out your hands, but, bowing low in a posture of worship and reverence you say: 'Amen' then wait for the prayer and give thanks to God....

It can be easily detected, that St. Cyril is instructing his listeners by employing a conversational tone; there is a blending of symbolism, directive and doctrine. The position of the deacon — as liaison is ever more pronounced. The believers' body postures and gestures all contribute to a prayerful expression of an inward faith. The sacred text again directs or suggests the formula that accompanies the liturgical action.

There is an interesting account of St. Cyril's generosity and the trouble it caused him recorded in the *Ecclesiastical History* of Sozomen. There is a feeling of enmity between Cyril and another bishop, Acacius. The following incident seemed to be a legitimate reason for contriving to depose Cyril. When there was a famine in Jerusalem, the poor sought help from Cyril, their bishop. Having no money on hand for them, Cyril sold for this purpose the veil and other sacred furnishings of the church. A certain individual recognized an offering which was presented to the altar by him as forming part of a costume of an actress. After investigating as to how it reached the stage, it was revealed that a merchant had sold it to the actress, and that Cyril had sold it to the merchant. With this pretext against Cyril, his accusers saw fit to exile him, and so a stage event was his coup de grace.[66] One is left wondering how that certain believer learned of the stage wardrobe! A variation of the same incident appears in the *Ecclesiastical History*, Book II, Chapter XXIII of Theodoret, 450 A.D. His writings take up where Eusebius leaves off. The account reads:

> "…And not least was Constantius moved by what was alleged against Cyril "for," said Acadius, "the holy robe, which the illustrious Constantine the emperor, in his desire to honour the church of Jerusalem, gave to Macarius, the bishop of that city, to be worn when he performed the rite of divine baptism, all fashioned with golden threads as it was, has been sold by Cyril. It has been bought," he continued, "by a certain stage dancer; dancing about when he was wearing it, he fell down and perished. With a man like this Cyril," he went on, "they set themselves up to judge and decide for the rest of the world…"

It may be worthwhile to observe the presence of the theatre in Jerusalem at this time. The city must have been cosmopolitan in its own right, for it is in the Jerusalem Church that we find first mention of vestments, use of incense at the gospel, and carrying of lights during the services. Cyril is very conscious of the fact that his own church is in the historical locale, where these events are dramatically commemorated in the liturgy. By the time of Etheria's pilgrimage we find a whole cycle of historical commemorations fully

---

[66] Sozomen, a Greek church historian (d.c. 450 at Constantinople) records this incident in Book IV, Chapter XXV of his *Ecclesiastical History*.

developed at Jerusalem, so that returning pilgrims told of the ceremonies they witnessed in the areas known to Jesus; as a result liturgical usage in many distant areas was deeply influenced.

E.   *Egeria's Pilgrimage* c. 385 A.D.

The work *Peregrinatio Aetheriae*, discovered in Arezzo, Italy in 1884 by the Italian archaeologist, G. F. Gamurrini, is one of the most important and interesting documents of the fourth century. This diary style account gives one the spot accounts of the Jerusalem liturgy, observing also the appropriateness of the prayers to the festival and place where the ceremony is held. Unlike the Wife of Bath, Egeria is considered to be a member of a religious community of women living in Galicia, Spain; it is for their edification that she writes this journal. However, like the Wife of Bath, she manifests a desire for visiting more shrines. Some of her comments will benefit our understanding of the relationship between the liturgical text and its actualization. She records Vespers, thus:

> "...At four o'clock they have 'Lychnicon' as they call it, or in our language — 'Lucernare'. All the people congregate once more in the Anastasis (Church of the Resurrection), and the lamps and candles are all lit. The fire is brought not from outside, but from the cave — inside the railings (cancellos) — where a lamp is always burning. For some time they have the Lucernare psalms and antiphons. Then they send for the bishop, who enters and sits in the main seat. The priests also enter and sit in their places, the hymns and antiphons go on. Then, when they have finished singing everything that was appointed, the bishop rises and goes in front of the railing. One of the deacons makes the normal commemoration of individuals and each time he mentions a name, a large group of boys responds Kyrie Eleison. The deacon calls every Catechumen to stand where he is and bow his head, and the bishop says the blessing over the Catechumens from his place. There is another prayer, after which the deacon calls for the faithful to bow their head, and the bishop says the blessing over them from his place. The dismissal takes place and they all come up one by one to kiss the bishop's hand.[67]

---

[67]   Passages from J. Wilkinson's *Egeria's Travels* and L. Duchesne's *Christian Worship,* (Latin and English version), SPCS, London, 1956.

She observes that the singing was appointed, i.e. the selection and length was determined before hand. This would indicate a fixed text and most likely a definite melody. In this selection Egeria sounds a bit like a theatre critic.

> "… What I found most impressive about all this was that the psalms and antiphons they use are always appropriate, whether at night, in the early morning, at the day prayers at midday or three o'clock, or at Lucernare. Everything is suitable appropriate and relevant to what is being done."[68]

Egeria's keen observation and interest in local setting is clearly preserved for us in her descriptions of the church in Jerusalem.

> "… And on this day in this church, and at the Anastasis and the Cross and Bethlehem, the decorations really are too marvelous for words. All you can see is gold and jewels and silk; the hangings are entirely silk with gold stripes, the curtains (cortinas) the same, and everything they use for services at the festival is made of gold and jewels. You simply cannot imagine the number, and the sheer weight of the candles and tapers and lamps and everything else they use for the services.
>
> They are beyond description, and so is the magnificent building itself…the decorations and rejoicing continue for eight days in all these places I have mentioned."[69]

What a feast for Western eyes this Oriental display must have been. The amount of luster and brilliance surely left an impression on her. A perfect setting for a serious celebration — a drama. No wonder the charitable gesture of St. Cyril, when he sold such furnishings, caused a slight claim to victory for his accusers. There must have been vestments worn by the clergy which enhanced the liturgy. Although Egeria doesn't mention any such clothing we read in Theodoret' *Ecclesiastical History*, Book II, Chapter 23:

> "…Constantine, the emperor, gave Macarius, the bishop of Jerusalem, a holy robe which was to be worn when he performed the

---

[68]   J. Wilkinson, *Egeria's Travels*, Chapter 25, line 4.
[69]   Op. cit.

rite of baptism. All fashioned with golden threads, was sold by Cyril. It had been bought by a certain stage dancer, who while dancing about while wearing it, fell down and perished."

The material worth of these garments was no doubt considerable, their worth also lay in their being suitable for such an awesome celebration. Egeria speaks of factors which make so fine a performance, all senses take part of this religious drama. In one section she reports of the incense filled church — the aromatic smoke added to a dramatic setting for the faithful's reflection on the Resurrection account:

"... After these three psalms and prayers they take censers into the cave of Anastasis, so that the whole Anastasis basilica is filled with the smell. Then the bishop, standing inside the screen, takes the Gospel book and goes to the door, where he himself reads the account of the Lord's resurrection"[70]

Egeria informs that there was the commemoration of the child Jesus to the temple, better known as the Presentation. This was celebrated forty days after Epiphany. It was to the temple in that very city that Jesus was presented. It is in writing such accounts as these to her community in Western Europe, that one grasps the meaning of the word: 'appropriate' in her journal. Egeria gives the account thus:

'On that day, there is a procession (processio) to the Church of the Resurrection and all gather there (procedunt). All things are done orderly with great joy, as at Easter. All the priests preach, then the bishop treating the event from the Gospel account about Joseph and Mary taking Jesus into the Temple...When all the things were orderly celebrated by customs, they celebrated the sacrament and thus departed (aguntur sacramenta, et sic fit missa)."[71]

Here one can almost visualize the development of this Gospel text into the more elaborate Mystery Plays. The raw material here is the nucleus, the bare essentials from which will develop the intricate pageants of the Middle Ages. One will also observe the Latin word: *missa*, the name which will

---

[70] Op. cit., Ch. 24, 1. 10.
[71] L. Duchesne, *Christian Worship*, p. 498, author's translation.

designate the Lord's Supper, in Western Europe and in its use in the Romance languages for future centuries.

A. *Palm Sunday*

'On this Sunday', she continues, 'when the service is over in the usual way, before the dismissal, the deacon makes this mention':

> 'During this week, starting tomorrow, let us meet at three in the afternoon at the Martyrium', then he says again: 'Let us be ready on the Eleona (Mt. of Olives) today at one o'clock.'

She continues:

> "At one o'clock all the people go up to the Church on Mount of Olives. The bishop takes his seat, and they have hymns and antiphons suitable to the place and the day and readings too...At five o'clock the passage is read from the Gospel about the children who met the Lord with palm branches...at this the bishop and all the people rise from their places and start off on foot down from the summit of the Mount of Olives. All the people go before him with psalms and antiphons, all the time repeating 'Blessed is he that comes in the name of the Lord.' The babies and the ones too young to walk are carried on their parents' shoulders. Everyone is carrying branches, some palm others olive and they accompany the bishop in the very way the people did when once they went down with the Lord. They go on foot all the way down the Mount to the city and throughout the city to the Church of the Resurrection, but they go rather slowly because of the older women and men among them who might get tired, so they reach the church rather late. Even though it is late, they celebrate the Lucernare when they get there, then are dismissed after a prayer."[72]

The beginning of Holy Week is the re-enactment of Jesus entry into Jerusalem with shouts of joy and palm branches used to meet the Lord. The deacon seems to have the fixed function of informing the laity as to where and when of the services. Egeria's eyes seem to take in all details — those in

---

[72] J. Wilkinson, op. cit., Chapters 30-31

the procession, the young, the old, their route through the city. This ceremony would later influence the Middle Age liturgy, and contribute as the kernel for the religious dramas. We seem to read a blueprint in Egeria's work. This day would become in later centuries, one of the major contributory factors in drama. The processions to sacred rites recall the narratives of the Gospel accounts. At that early period, the cycle of historical commemorations seem fully organized and developed.

B. *Holy Thursday*

"...before the dismissal the deacon announces:

'Let us meet tonight at seven o'clock in the Church on the Mt. of Olives. There is a great task awaiting us tonight.'

... then everybody hurries home for a meal, when finished they return to the church, there they continue to sing hymns suitable to the place and the day...about midnight they leave and go up with hymns to the place from which the Lord ascended into heaven. And there they again have readings and hymns and antiphons suitable to the day, and the prayers which the bishop says are all appropriate to the day and to the place."[73]

Again we hear the deacon giving directives. Although Egeria repeats her awareness of the suitable prayer at the proper site, she never mentions the Washing of the Feet — a ceremony that was added to the Liturgy much later in time. One must remember that the bare essentials are mentioned by Egeria. She continues:

"Then the bishop and all the people go into a church which has been built here (Gethsemane) and have a prayer appropriate to the place and day (oratio apta loco et diei)...Next they go with singing to the city, and reach the gate...thus the bishop is conducted from Gethsemane... after the Gospel reading, the passage about the Lord being led away to Pilate...the bishop speaks a word of encouragement to the

---

[73] Op. cit., Chapter 35.

people...he tells them not to be weary...when he has given them as much encouragement as he can, he speaks to them thus:

'Now go home each one of you till the next service, sit and rest a bit, then be back here about eight o'clock so that till midday you can see the holy Wood of the Cross...and give our minds to readings and prayers till nightfall.'"

Chapter 37 continues:

"...it is not long before everyone is assembled for the next service. The bishop's chair is placed...and he takes his seat (cathedra). A table is placed before him with a cloth on it, the deacons stand around the table, and there is brought to him a gold and silver box containing the holy Wood of the Cross. It is opened and the Wood and the Title are taken out and placed on the table.

As long as the holy Wood is on the table, the bishop sits with his hands resting on either end of it and holds it down, and the deacons round him keep watch over it...all the people go past one by one. They stoop down, touch the Wood first with their forehead and then kiss it, but no one puts out his hand to touch it...the place is so c-rammed with people...between noon and three o'clock there are readings about the things that Jesus suffered, first the psalms on this subject, then the Epistles and Acts which concern it, then passages from the Gospel Thus they read the prophecies about what the Lord would suffer...between the reading are prayers, all of them appropriate a prayer, and the dismissal."

The Good Friday Liturgy is rather familiar, yet it lacks certain elements we now have. The main feature then as now is the Adoration of the Cross; both the Trisagion and 'Procession to the Tomb' came many year later. Perhaps the most intimate form of lay involvement was, as Egeria mentions in Chapter 37, line 7: "it is impressive to see the way all the people are m-oved by the readings, and how they mourn. You could hardly believe how every single one of them weeps during the three hours, old and young alike, because of the manner in which the Lord suffered for us."

The fact that the liturgy was simple and concise, did not prevent the laity from participating to an extent. Close to the end of her travel memoirs, Egeria tells us that when the bishop relates what has been done (Baptism), and interprets it, as he does so, the applause is so loud that it can be heard outside the church. It is interesting to connect this type of applause with the applause that will be heard centuries later — not in the church, as much as in the theatre.

V
Reconciliation of Penitents

As the Church continued, and expressed its belief in the teachings of Christ, annual feasts commemorating His redemptive activity became more fixed and expressive of the mystery that was being celebrated. Pope Innocent I (d. 417 A.D.) is well attributed with formulating this axiom 'Lex orandi, lex credendi': the law of praying is the law of believing. In fact it means that the external worship, or actualized prayer is the on the surface expression of belief. In other words prayer (liturgy) is the external presentation of the belief (inner conviction) of the Christian. Here is found the notion which is analogous to the idea of script serving as the starting point for actualization. In the present era, rewording the same idea by saying 'from text to performance' would seem appropriate at this point.

Church's Position — Theological Basis

It is a known fact that the Church believed that sins committed after Baptism could be forgiven in the sacrament of Penance. The early Christians were well aware that there could be members of their community who were sinners. The individual who sinned (a grave sin warranted a public reconciliation) would have to do public penance and then be reconciled with the Church and with God. A special liturgy developed to bring out this penitential mood. Various outlines and formulae found their way into the Church's liturgy, using as their primary directives the accounts in scripture that deal with this prayer expression. The penitential ritual began once the confession of sin was made to the bishop or to the priest, and lasted to an appointed time set to the bishops discretion. During this time, the penitent was forbidden to associate with the community for public prayer and worship. After deceiving a hairshirt from the celebrant, the penitent left for a place of seclusion to perform his allotted penance. Later, it was that this penance period began on Ash Wednesday and lasted until Holy Thursday. By the end of the sixth century, this public type of penance gave way to the private form of reconciliation, known as private confession. Nevertheless, public penance did express outwardly the inner beliefs of the faithful; supported by the scriptures and texts of Church writers. This ritual did impress the people of that time by serving as a channel for dramatic expression. This impulse contributed much to further the development of drama in the following centuries.

Old Testament Basis

To better understand this penitential setting, one must turn to the Old Testament descriptions in presenting the actualization of an inner belief. Job tells us how he performs an external penance after speaking so foolishly about God.

Job Chapter 42: 1, 2, 6

"Then Job answered the Lord and said: I know that you can do all things and that no purpose of yours can be hindered...therefore I disown what I have said, and repent in dust and ashes.

Similarly, David expressed his inner sorrow for sin:

2 Samuel 12: 13...

"Then David said to Nathan: "I have sinned against the Lord...he kept a fast, retiring for the night to lie on the ground clothed in sackcloth. The elders of his house stood beside him urging him to rise from the ground, but he would not, nor would he take food...rising from the ground. David washed and anointed himself and changes his clothes. The he went to the house of the Lord and worshipped.'"

One can read another instance of repentance carried out with external performance in:

Jonah 3:5...

"...when the people of Nineveh believed God, they proclaimed a
fast and all of them, great and small, put on sackcloth — when the
news reached the king of Nineveh, he rose from his throne, laid aside
his robe, covered himself with sackcloth, and sat in the ashes. Then he
had this proclaimed: 'neither man nor beast shall taste anything...man
and beast shall be covered with sackcloth and call loudly to God.'"

There is a call for that inner change of heart accompanied by an inner
expressions here too the idea is quite clear — as expressed in:

Joel 2:12, 15, 17

"Yet even now, says the Lord, return to me with your whole heart,
with fasting, arid weeping and mourning, rend your hearts, not your
garmentst and return to the Lord...

What follows seems to be the natural dramatic expression:

"Blow the trumpet in Zion! Proclaim a fast, call an assembly, gather the
people...between the porch and the altar let the priests, the ministers
of the Lord, weep, and say: "Spare, O Lord, your people..."'"

Patristic Period

A.   Tertullian

The Christians soon adopted the penitential expression of the Old Testament for there was an ever more awareness of man's need to respond to the
call of the Father through His Son, Jesus Christ. The prolific writer of the early Church, Tertullian, recounts in his work *De Penitentia* (On Repentance) c.
198 A.D., Chapter IX:

"...This act (not only exhibited in the conscience alone but carried out in some external act as well) is spoken of whereby we confess our sins to the Lord... repentence is born. Thus 'exomologesis' is a discipline for man's prostration and humiliation to move mercy. With regard to the very dress and food, It commands (the penitent) to lie in sackcloth and ashes,...to bow before the feet of the presbyters and kneel to God's dear ones...all this 'exomologesis' enhances repentance. Therefore, while it abases, it raises up; while it covers with squalor it renders clean....

Chapter X

"...Yet most men either shun this work, as being a public exposure of themselves or else defer it from day to day...is it better to be damned in secret than absolved in public?. what if besides the shame which they make the most account of, men dread likewise the bodily inconveniences... they must spend their time in the roughriess of sackcloth, and the horridness of ashes...is it then becoming for us to supplicate for our sins in scarlet and purple?"

Although Tertullian speaks of the doctrinal aspect of repentance, he does mention the practical element of dealing with the shame that the sinner dreads, this very shame caused by the public manifestation of what should be going on in his conscience. Underlying this 'exomologesis' is the believer's desire to make restitution for any evil committed in his life. Tertullian is also curt in regard to any ritual that accompanied these gestures. Perhaps he is too emphatic in treating the doctrinal importance of repentance, while the other possibility (which seems more likely the reason) is that it is too early of a stage in Church history for an elaborate or ceremonial reception of sinners to have been developed, polished and enhanced with ritual.

We find evidence of a public expression of sorrow with the textual foundation for its very source. Other sources reveal to us the situation at that time.

B.   *Sozomen* 324-425 A.D.

Recorded, in his *Ecclesiastical History*, Chapter XVI, is this scene:

"It is observed with great rigor by the Western churches, particularly at Rome, where there is a place appropriated to the deception of penitentst in which spot they stand and mourn until the completion of the services, for it is not lawful for them to take part in the mysteries; then they cast themselves, with groans and lamentations, prostrate on the ground. The bishop conducts the ceremony, sheds tears, and prostrates himself in like manner and all the people burst into tears, and groan aloud. Afterwards, the bishop rises first from the ground, and raises up the others; he offers up prayer on behalf of the penitents, and then dismisses them. Each of the penitents subjects himself in private to voluntary suffering, either by fastings, by abstaining from the bath or from diverse kinds of meats, or by other prescribed means, until a certain period appointed by the bishop. Then the time arrives, he is made free from the consequences of his sin, and assembles at the church with the people. The Roman priests have carefully observed this custom from the beginning to the present time.

C. *Synod of Laodicea* c. 363 A.D.

Canon XIX

"After the sermons...the prayer for the Catechumens is to be made... after the Catechumens have gone out, the prayer for those who are under penance: after these have passed under the hand of the bishop, and departed, there should then be offered the three prayers of the faithful..."

D. *Apostolic Constitutions* c. 380 A.D.

Book VII, Chapter IX

The prayer fo the penitents reads:

"...Look down upon these persons who have bended the neck of their soul and body to Thee...restore them to your holy Church, into their former dignity and honor..." Then let the deacon say:

"Depart you penitents, let none of those who ought not to come draw

71

near. All we of the faithful, let us bend our knees: let us all entreat God..."

There seems to be more of a ritual in this instance. The role of the deacon is rather pronounced. As in the other parts of the liturgy, the deacon, as a secondary character of a drama, sets the relationship between the audience and main character. It is quite evident that a bond is established by the deacon's plea to prayer: the celebrant sums up the prayer of the faithful, in behalf of the penitents.

E. *Synod of Hippo* — 383 A.D.

a. *Canon XXV*

"If an offense is publicly known, the penitent shall receive the imposition of hands before apsis, i.e. in public."

Development and Contents of the Rite for Penitents

One reads of the rudimentary development from simple to a more complex actualization of the penitentiary rite — a major factor toward this development was surely the various church councils. Many canons, found in the code of these councils, mention the various bodily position of the penitents during their time spent at public worship. As early as the fourth century one finds four penitential stations.[75] In reading their description, one becomes aware of the penitents' role, as characters in a play.

The first class consisted of the very severe offenders: (Mourners — Flentes — προσκλαιοντες). They stood outside the door of the church, in what we would call the church yard. It was there that the 'mourners' implored the faithful to allow them to be admitted to penance at all. During a period of time, they were expected to present themselves outside the church door, and give proofs of their good intentions, by wearing sackcloth and ashes, shaving

---

[75] The following information is interesting to read in the book by R.S.T. Haslehurst, *Penitential Discipline in the Early Church*, MacMillan, London, 1921, pp. 88-91.

their heads, women would veil their heads, and both implored the prayers of the faithful.

The second class was those allowed within the church building itself. Assembled in the narthex they (Hearers — Audientes — αχϱοωμενοι) would listen to the reading of the scriptures and homily.

The third group, that of Kneelers (Substrati — υποπιποντες) were permitted to meet within the door of the church, but left with the catechumens. These were those who were mentioned above in Canon XIX of the Synod of Laodicea. They received the benefit of special prayers and the imposition of hands.

The fourth group the Standers (Consistentes — συνισταμενοι), whose position was with the faithful, beyond the ambo and probably in the rear of the actual communicants.

Reading of these various individuals in church documents with their prescribed attire and position in the church and its area, reminds one of reading the list of the characters of a drama, and their specific role on stage plus the distinctive attire — all contributed to an awesome spectacle. An account of such public display is recorded in the works of the church historian, Sozomen. He mentions that this custom still prevailed with great rigor in Rome, where there was a place appropriated to the reception of penitents, in which spot they stood and mourned and waited for the end of the liturgy at which point they prostrated themselves with groans and lamentations, they even shed tears, while the people in the assembly, to show their fellowship with them joined their tears and raised their mournful sighs with theirs. The celebrant rose first and offered a prayer for the penitents, who after promising to perform some form of public or private penance, leave the assembly. After a period of time, the penitents may regain their rank with the faithful.[76]

Another interesting incident is recorded in Chapter XXV:

> When the Emperor Theodosius approached the entrance of the Church in Milan, he was met by Ambrose, the bishop of the city, 'who took hold of him by his purple robe' and reprimanded him for the useless slaughter at Thessalonica. No entry was allowed into the church or attendance at the Liturgy without first repentance. The emperor was impressed by the whole confrontation, admired Ambrose's reaction, and reflected on his own wrongdoings. After being forbidden to enter

---

[76] Sozomen, *Church History*, VII, 16.

the church, Theodosius confessed his sin publicly and during his allotted period of penance, refused to wear his imperial ornaments.

There is certainly a dramatic element in this situation — the emperor, as the main character, performs a public act penance publicly in the view of all, as on stage. Setting aside his royal clothes, as though they were the costume, he changes his role now as the one who performs penance. His accompanying body gestures also heighten the tensity of the whole outcome. The motion of gestures taken in a penitential setting will be of interest.

One will notice that a theological appraisal of public confession and public penance or public penance and private confession, will not be treated. One's attention, rather will be focused on the overall ceremony with its dramatic overtones and potential for dramatization. The ritual had a theatrical atmosphere (using the word 'theatre' in the modern sense).

E. *Penitential Gestures*

It would be important at this point to mention the various postures of the body which, in this case, enhanced the attitude of penance and compunction. From the earliest times of Christianity, gestures accompanied with words formed a valid prayer expression.

a) *Kneeling — Genuflection*

Kneeling is a natural body posture which spurs the notion of seeking pardon and forgiveness. The scriptures attest to its use.[77] The mention of kneeling is found in the works of the early church writers.[78] This expression of penance became associated with the reconciliation ceremony of penitents. The format of this prayer is arranged thus:

the celebrant invites the assembly to pray — 'Oremus'

the deacon give the directive to kneel and privately express sentiments — 'Flectamus genua'

---

[77] 1 Kings 8:54; 19:18; Ps 95:6; Luke 22:41; Acts 9:40.
[78] Tertullian, *On Prayer*, 14; *Shepherd of Hermas*, Dream I, Ch. 3; St. Clement of Itome, his letter to the Corinthians, Ch. 57:1,2; Sozomen's *Church History*, Bk. I, Ch. 7, 1. 16.

after a while the deacon cries out the directive to rise — 'Levate'

the celebrant then addresses the particular petition to God — 'Deus, qui etc...'

Alcuin (c. 790 A.D.) also mentions this expression of penance as the posture for private confession at his time.[79]

b)   *Striking of Breast*

This gesture likewise expresses a contrite heart, and the guilt that the penitent is aware of — it is that guilt he wishes to have removed and replaced with a renewed and clean heart. It is during the period of penance that God would create that new heart for the penitent. St. Augustine reports in his Sermon 351,[80] that the celebrant and faithful struck their breasts as the words in the Lord's Prayer: 'Forgive us our sins.' In this natural gesture of a penitential spirit the penitent acknowledged his sorrow and displeasure for the evil performed, and at the same time expressed his intention to satisfy for his sins. The texts found in St. Luke 18:13, and 23:48 seem to sum up the whole penitential motif.

c)   *Inclination of the Head — Bows*

The penitential aspect of this body posture was associated with the blessings bestowed upon the penitents before they left the community of worshipers. One reads already in the *Apostolic Constitutions*, the bishop's gesture of imposing his hands over the penitents as a blessing. The deacon cried out the directive:

'Incline, or Humiliate capita vestra Deo'. —
'Bow your head before God'.

The celebrant then prayed the prayer over the people (oratio super populum). This gesture surely evokes a penitential mood. This humble bow is made whenever a blessing is granted.[81]

---

[79]   PL 101, 1194.
[80]   PL 39, 1541: Sermon 67 also refers to this gesture.
[81]   See Genesis 24:48; Chronicles 29:20.

d) *Prostration*

This gesture is employed by Abraham in awe, as he worshiped God (Gen. 17:3).[82] One reads that Jesus fell prostrate in Gethsemane, during His sufferings (Matt 26:39). Tertullian mentions in his *On Penance* that this gesture is a form of penance, as was seen above. Sozomen, the 5th century church historian, describes the penitential scene of penitents and bishop at the end of Mass, to beg God's forgiveness (Church History VII:16). This same body position always retained the idea of penance; it is still used today at the Good Friday liturgy as well as at ordinations and at various blessings.

Other gestures, like a spoken language, convey to the viewer a message or meaning. In many instances, these gestures and other actions were interpreted according to one's norms rather than to a set of norms of commentary: such activity was to help set the scene for the Middle Age liturgy and its inter-relationship with local factors in producing liturgical drama.

The whole penitential theme is vividly expressed in *Joel*

2:13 'Rend your hearts, not your garments, and return to the Lord...'

2:15 'Blow the trumpet in Zion! Proclaim a fast, call an assembly...'

2:16 'Gather the people, notify the congregation, assemble the elders...'

2:17 Between the porch and the altar let the priests, the ministers of the Lord weep, and say, 'Spare, O Lord, your people and make not your heritage a reproach...'

One notices in this passage a directive which is uttered in faith, a description of various gestures for the hearers to emulate and thereby share in the penance which is exhorted to all, and all this is based on their belief attested to by the text. The liturgy, in this way, uses actions to instruct and teach. Word and gesture produces a dramatic element, moreover, during this time in history, while the various church councils are discouraging association with the theater etc..., yet the Church itself is indirectly encouraging the dramatic

---

[82] Cf. Luke 17:16 '...the Samaritan threw himself on his face at the feet of Jesus.'

element in her very ceremonies. The ritual performed for the reception of penitents is a clear case of 'Lex orandi lex credendi'.

F.   The Rite Itself

The following descriptions of the prayers and ceremonies will help us visualize the penitents' public act of being reinstated in the community of believers. Limiting our scope to the Western Church, we are fortunate to read of this ceremony in the Gelasian Sacramentary.[83]

G.   Variations with Dramatic Overtones

a)   *Roman* (Usage)

The final day of penance arrived for the penitent — from the beginning of Lent, Ash Wednesday until Holy Thursday, the penitent was to perform some type of penance. Now, reconciliation on Holy Thursday made it possible for the penitent to celebrate the Easter Triduum, i.e. Holy Thursday, Good Friday, Easter Vigil and Easter day, together with the whole community.

The Sacramentary records for us that:

> the penitent comes into the church from where he was performing penance and prostrates (omni corpore in terra) full length in the church. The deacon addresses the celebrant in these words:
> "Adest, o venerabilis pontifex, tempus acceptum...' (This is the acceptable time...)

As the secondary character in a drama, the deacon continues to speak in behalf of the penitents so that pardon may be granted.

A prayer is said over the penitents. The celebrant then admonishes each penitent, lays hands on his head, bids him rise...the Mass continues.[84]

---

[83]   Most ancient Roman liturgical books, completed between 628-731 A.D. Very unlikely that Pope Gelasius (492-496 A.D.) composed the entire work — whence its name. PL 74, 1095...

[84]   cf. Msgr. L. Duchesne, *Christian Worship*, pp. 439-41. Josef A. Jungmann,

b) *Toledo* (Usage)

Among the many distinct peculiarities of the Mozarabic Liturgy is the one of reconciliation of penitents on Good Friday and not on Holy Thursday. This ceremony, known as *Indulgentia* was already prescribed by the fourth Council of Toledo in 633 A.D. The very wording of Canon VI indicates the liturgical proclamation of the redemptive act of Jesus Christ. His death brings forgiveness and pardon to all. Herein lies the reason for this ceremony on Good Friday.[85] The format of the text, following the *Improperia*, a dialogue between Christ and His people, based on the words of Micah 6, sets an emotional high pitch of the day's events. No doubt the seed of a dramatized sermon is before us, and rightly so, for the Lord wished to have this event preached, proclaimed, made known — praedicare. After several verses of Psalms, the pleas for silence was echoed:

Silentium facite!

Then followed further directives with an invitation to prayer:

'Pray penitents, kneel before Our God.' Let us pray to Our Lord that He grant you pardon (indulgentiam) and remission for all your sins. Let us beseech Our Lord. After our prayer is completed, let us with an equal voice seek pardon from Our Lord.'

Then, while prostrated, they would seek pardon as much as 300 times! After this emotional prayer, the prayer to the Good shepherd was presented:

'You, Good shepherd, gave your life for Your sheep'

The deacon prayed:

'We pray You, O Lord, that you grant us remission for our sins, and peace.'

New cries of *Indulgentia* were again begun:

S.J., *The Early Liturgy*, pp. 241-43. Cyrille Vogel, *La Discipline Penitentielle en Gaule*, pp. 183-86, French text, Latin prayers.

[85]'Oportet eidem die mysterium crucis...praedicare atque indulgentiam criminum clara voce omnem populum postulare...

Te precamur, Domine — Indulgentia
Procedat ab Altissimo — Indulgentia
Succurat nobis miseris — Indulgentia
Delicta purget omnibus — Indulgentia
Lapsos peccatis erigat — Indulgentia
Te precamur, Domine — Indulgentia

A third time, after the prayers, the cries *Indulgentia* are made afresh but may exceed not more than 100 times! The celebrant then kneels at the steps of the altar and prays:

'Pray O penitents, kneel before God and seek remission for your sins and peace. Rise in the name of Christ, and when your prayer is complete answer together. Amen.

A final directive ended this part of the Good Friday liturgy:

'State locis vestris ad Missam.'
(Remain in your places...)[86]

Eliminating the intricate historical modifications which shaped this ceremony the reader will remain content to learn that the basic element of faith which underlies the whole ceremony is the proclaiming of the Lord's suffering and the pardon for sin are dramatically presented as one event, in one celebration. One will also be aware of the sense of relief for the faithful, the catharsis for the audience, as it were; the fact that during the 'drama', their sins are forgiven. There is little wonder, then, that the earliest plays centered around this part of faith — man's salvation through the Lord's Pascal Mystery.

c) *Abbot Regino of Prum*

About 906, Regino compiled his work *Ecclesiastical Discipline* at the bidding of Rathbod, archbishop of Trier. Among the many regulations included in the work, is one which deals with penitents on Ash Wednesday. He gives directives for the acceptance of penitents.

---

[86] PL 86, 612-13.

On Ash Wednesday the penitents shall present themselves to the bishop at the church doors. They are clad in sackcloth bare feet and downcast eyes reveal their guilt Penances are measured out according to each one's guilt. Led into the church, they will prostrate themselves upon the floor, during which time the penitential psalms were chanted by the clergy. Later they rise and are sprinkled with holy water. After they received ashes on their heads and were covered with sackcloth, they are cast out from the Church, during the responsory: 'In the sweat of thy face shall you eat bread...' On Holy Thursday, they shall be presented at the threshold of the Church."[87]

Such harsh and severe treatment would perhaps shock the reader. One must keep in mind, that the ceremony was public, and the bystanders must had been equally brought to a sense of compunction. To leave one with the impression that this is all that happened would be falsifying the fact. The reader will see that this severity was meted with equal compassion and tenderness.

d) *Roman Pontifical — XII Century*

The ceremony for the reception of penitents is most moving, religious, as well as dramatic. The sense of one spectacle is clearly maintained by word and action. There is an identification of celebrant, ministers and faithful which constitutes an expression of an unfolding drama — a welcoming, a homecoming.

'At the third hour (9 A.M.) the ministers enter the church. The celebrant, seated outside the main entrance of the church listens to the penitents' plea for entry.

The deacon requests that the penitent be received, a long prayer concludes with the sentiment that the grace of penance is one, and profits each one who receives it and gives help to all in common.

Then the celebrant himself, prostrated before all present prays a scriptural quote:

---

[87] PL 132:241.

Turn your face from my sins, Lord...

The deacon then requests that the penitent be accepted for it was by human weakness that a believer was lured by the evil one.

The celebrant says: 'Come! With the deacon's invitation to kneel, the rest of the penitents make their way up the name of the church. At each request to come, the penitents move closer to the chancel where now the celebrant eagerly awaits them. At the threefold *Venite* — Come, the penitents race up to the celebrant, who at this time is reciting the words from the psalm: Come, children, listen to me, I will teach you the fear of the Lord: after this is sung the psalm: I will bless the Lord at all times... let the penitents be handed to the deacon and by him to the celebrant, and by Him be restored to the bosom of the church. Soon the litany is chanted, during which the celebrant prostrates himself with the penitents!

The Lord's Prayer is said together with several prayers addressed to God with such sentiments as: We offer you our sorrow. Spare those who believe in You, Absolve us, your sheep, O Good Shepherd. The assembly is by now solidified, and the penitents are referred to as brothers. Reassuring them of their dignity and eternal worth, they are blessed by the celebrant with holy water to the words: 'Arise you who sleep, may Christ enlighten you! The bells are then rung and the Mass of the day continues...'[88]

H.   Concluding Remark

a)   *St. Thomas Aguinas, D. 1275*

As far as St. Thomas was concerned, the subject of public penance was worthy of mention. He describes public penance in almost the same words as its description read in the above selection. In answer to the question: 'Whether a solemn penance can be repeated?' St. Thomas maintains that it ought not be repeated for three reasons: first, frequency may lead into contempt; secondly because of its signification — the expulsion of Adam from

---

[88]   Michel Andrieu, *Le Pontifical Romain Au Moyen-Age* Tome I, Vatican 1938, pp. 215-219.

paradise, which happened only once; thirdly, because the solemnization indicates that a believer makes a profession of continual repentance, and repetition is inconsistent with solemnization.[89]

It seems quite clear that the rites of public penance were well established at this time and their use supported by the teaching of the church's philosophers and theologians, as voiced in the work of St. Thomas Aquinas. As a result, not only did the rite have a dramatic element to it, but also the theological rationale which supported it, and encouraged its usage.

INGREDIENTS OF DRAMATIC SETTING IN PENITENTS RITE

	Celebrant	*Penitent*	*Faithful*
Actors	Primary Character, celebrant, secondary character — deacons	actors, cast	spectators
Stage	Sanctuary porch, chancel	portico chancel	nave
Costume	Vestments	sackcloth	street attire
Gestures	Standing, sitting	kneeling, prostrating	walking, standing
Verbal Expression	Monologue	dialogue	response, chorus

---

[89] *Summa Theologica* III, Supl. q. 28, a.2;3.

VI
Dedication of Churches

The very nature of worship for both the people of ancient Israel as well as the Christians included the public gathering of the believers. For the Israelites, the Temple was the most holy place on earth because it was the dwelling place of the Lord (Psalm 84). The Temple served as the place for public prayer and sacrifice. It was indeed an awesome area and a holy place. The very center of the people's religion was anchored at the Temple.

The advent of Christianity shifted the dwelling place of the Lord from the Temple to the individual believer (1 Corinthians 6:19). Both faiths believed God was everywhere, but faith included the idea that the believer may worship God in a certain place. During the early centuries of persecution, Christians worshipped at tombs of martyrs, which were located in the suburbs.[90] One reads in Acts 3:46 that the early Christians attended prayers at the Temple but reserved the private homes of the believers for the 'Breaking of Bread'. As yet, there was no idea of a specific building for common worship, besides the atmosphere of persecution made it almost impossible for the faithful to erect a permanent place of worship. As a result, worship was left to the bare essentials in its construction. It seems evident that there was no immediate desire to dedicate a building for worship during the early years of Christianity. One is informed of solemn liturgical formulae for church dedications only after 313 A.D.!

It must be kept in mind that the medieval stage in Europe evolved as an educative means, through which the church through its liturgy, taught the

---

[90] St. Augustine, *Confessions* VI, ii.

very mysteries that were being celebrated. Initially, the dramatic ritual surrounding worship took place within the church building itself, eventually it became the outdoor theatre, popularized in many respects. Now, the church building itself with its chancel was very much equipped for the actualization of the ritual, insofar as the ritual, performed like a play, was shared by performer and audience. It has been noted that from ancient times, the deacon's main function in the ceremonies was to maintain that link between celebrant (main actor) and worshiper (audience).

Yet, the idea of selection and dedication of an area for worship with special ceremonies is evident from Scripture. We find interesting references made of the Temple dedication itself which for our purposes reveal a dramatic impulse.

A. Old Testament Sources

In Exodus 40, we read that Moses was given directives:

> 'to take the anointing oil and anoint the Dwelling and everything in it, consecrating it and all its furnishings...anoint the altar...the laver and thus consecrate it.

From this rudimentary rite, a more elaborate solemn one is developed by the time of King Solomon. Recorded for us in I Kings 8, is the lavish description of the Temple dedication:

> '...when Solomon finished this entire prayer he rose from before the altar, where he had been kneeling with his hands outstretched toward heaven...thus the king and all the Israelites dedicated the temple of the Lord. On that day the king consecrated the middle of the court facing the temple of the Lord; he offered there the holocausts...'

Mention is made of musicians in 2 Chronicles 5:12-14

> '...the Levites who were singers...clothed in fine linen, with cymbals, harps and lyres, stood east of the altar, and with them a hundred and twenty priests blowing trumpets. When the trumpeters and singers were heard as a single voice praising and giving thanks, and when they

raised the sound of the trumpets, cymbals and other musical instruments ...the building of the Lord's temple was filled with a cloud.'

Some Psalms refer to the Temple as the Lord's house containing a beauty that attracts the believers.[91] It is evident that there is a happiness for those who continuously praise the Lord. That worship consists in the performance of a daily prayer schedule — sacrifices, offerings of incense, and musical accompaniment — a very dramatic event indeed. Psalm 24 has all the ingredients for a dramatic effect:

'Lift up, O gates, your lintels;
    reach up, you ancient portals,
    that the king of glory may come in!
Who is the king of glory?
    The Lord strong and mighty,
    The Lord, mighty in battle
Lift up, O gates, your lintels, etc...
    The Lord of hosts; he is the king of
    glory.

This apostrophe which is addressed to the temple doors creates a high pitched mood for the entry of the king. Centuries later, these verses were to be incorporated into the rite of consecration for new churches. The verses were sung by a choir as a response to the celebrant's utterance or is a response to another choir. This antiphonal format became so much a part of the ceremony that, as a dramatic dialogue plue ceremonial miming, it was presented to the believers as something a very short play. We will treat more of this further on.

B. *Early Patristic Sources*
1) *Eusebius* — Father of Church History (c.265-c.340 A.D.)

There is a long panegyric delivered by Eusebius to Paulinus, a bishop of Tyre on the occasion of that city's Cathedral dedication in 314 A.D. Eusebius delivers a long sermon but tells us nothing of the rite of dedication itself. He speaks of the usual ingredients of worship and considers the dedication as

---

[91]   cf. Psalms 26, 42, 84, 122.

one whole ceremony of worship. This would not be surprising at all, for the Church at this time had no elaborate ritual for such events. Interestingly enough Eusebius notes:

> ...perfect services were conducted by the prelates, the sacred rites being solemnized, and the majestic institutions of the Church observed, here with the singing of psalms and with the reading of the word committed to us by God, and there with the performance of divine and mystic services; and the mysterious symbols of the Saviour's passion were dispensed. At the same time people of every age, both male and female, with all the power of the mind gave honor unto God, the author of their benefits, in prayers and thanksgiving, with a joyful mind and soul. And every one of the bishops present, each to the best of his ability, delivered orations, adding luster to the assembly.[92]

His lengthy sermon touches upon the architecture and furnishings of the basilica. Had Eusebius said half as much about the service as he said about the church itself with its adjacent buildings and rooms, courtyards and marble floors, we would have had a very good notion of the dedication ceremony of the early fourth century. Then again, one is not certain if there existed a dedication ceremony as such; nevertheless, the elements of drama were certainly present. This authentic account gives us an idea of a spectacle in a legitimate sense.

2)   *Egeria's Travels* — c. 385 A.D.

Egeria's scanty information tends to leave the reader with the inclination to accept the fact that a dedication ceremony did take place in Jerusalem during her pilgrimage there, but there is no mention of set ritual, ceremonies, or prayers. Nevertheless, one cannot conclude that there was a lack of dramatic activity during those holy days. Egeria informs her reader that on the day the Church of Golgotha was consecrated, the Church of the Resurrection was also consecrated. It was a feast of special magnificence, for it was on that very date when the cross of the Lord was discovered. Ceremonies were arranged to observe the happy event, with full joy for eight days. Neigh-

---

[92]   *Church History* X, 3-4 Nicene and Post Nicene Fathers, Vol. I, P. Schaff and H. Wace, pp. 370-378.

boring countries sent their monks, clergy and laity. Attendance was considered an obligation, It was not surprising to see at least fifty bishops present. The churches are decorated in the same way they are for Easter and Epiphany. On the first and second day of the festivities, the worshipers assemble at the one church, on the following days they are to gather at the other assigned churches...[93] while no specific prayers are mentioned, nor a ceremonial format is described, one will be safe to maintain the opinion that those days spent in prayers and ceremonies from one church to another, were surely full of elaborate ritual, which had a dramatic tone that made those moments of worship very awesome and impressive for all present. The lack of ritual text does not deny the presence of dramatization or actualization, at least Egeria's work offers support in this regard.

3) *Theodoret of Cyrus* — c. 386-458 A.D.

Another work which gives the account of the same Jerusalem Church, is found in Theodoret's *Church History* (450 A.D.). Similar to Egeria's account, this account doesn't mention any set ritual or format which was used in the dedication ceremony. However, the document furnishes us with the idea that the function was awesome. There is mention of the altar being decorated with royal hangings while the golden vessels were enhanced with gems. The emperor, who initiated the whole ceremony, was elated at the splendor and lavishness of the whole affair.[94]

The mention of objects and decorations would easily convey the idea of the equipment on stage employed during a presentation, while the awareness of the atmosphere of a festival would associate one's thoughts with that atmosphere which later surrounded the plays in the Middle Ages.

Soon after the conversion of Constantine, Christians were much freer in expressing their religious beliefs. There were no restrictions as to their ownership of property reserved for worship. In time as they grew, they developed a distant type of architecture which was already known as the basilica style; akin to the civil law courts, it soon was adapted for church use. The nave and side aisles lead to the apse, where the celebrant and other clergy had their specific places during the liturgy. In front of them and facing the people was the altar, unadorned and made of stone or wood. A canopy resting on four posts hovered over the altar. The worshipers stood in the nave facing the

---

[93]   John Wilkinson, *Egeria's Travels*, Chapters 48-49.
[94]   Theodoret, *Church History*, Bk. I, XXIX.

altar during the ceremonies. Before entering the church proper, the worshipers would first have to walk through the atrium, that place of peace and quiet off the streets serving as a vestibule to the church. Trees, flowers and a small pool of water afforded beauty. Such architecture rendered itself for the celebration of the liturgy. All was set as a stage — the celebrant with the clergy in the apse and the faithful before him with unobstructed view foreshadowed the stage arrangement of leading actor and audience. The liturgy celebrated in such a milieu had to be nothing but dramatic.

While the Roman influence fostered the aspect of the church to be viewed as a tomb, (more so the altar), on the other hand the Gallican approach was more dynamic. The church building itself was looked upon as a living entity, hence it had to be made worthy for the celebration of the liturgy. The preparation included the elements of washing and anointing, parallel to the Baptismal liturgy. As a result the building was rendered holy and worthy for the celebration of religious rites. The Church conveyed and taught this aspect of belief through ceremony and ritual which were full of artistic dramatization, and were surrounded in an impressive setting of awe. That which actually takes place in the Dedication Ceremony is the realization of the fact that the word or script is related to the external performance, i.e. the blessing of the structure.

It will be well now to note the mere elementary rite of dedication in the early years of the church, then to note the gradual additions of ritual which was paralleled in the secular arena by the laity's desire for a more dramatic expression.

C. Medieval Sources

1. *Pope Vigilius' Letter* — 538 A.D.

At least, up to two hundred years after Eusebius, it was quite evident that the dedication ceremony consisted in just the celebration of the Mass. Such evidence leading toward a usage is found in the letter of Pope Vigilius to the bishop of Braga, dated June 29, 538. The letter sent to bishop Profuturus makes it quite clear that there is no need to sprinkle the church with holy water, once Mass has been celebrated (nihil iudicamus officere si per eam minime aqua exorcizata iactetur). The reason for this directive is that the celebration of Mass constitutes the dedication itself (quia consecrationem... ecclesiae..celebritatem tantum scimus esse missarum).[95]

There was a popular devotion toward the martyrs. It was fostered easily because the laity loved to meet for liturgical services on the sites of their burials. Soon large shelters were built over the tombs of these martyrs. If, however, the relics of the particular martyr were not already in the edifice, they were brought to the new resting place amid pomp and ceremony.[96] Eventually the dedication became more elaborate and festive in tone. Some momentum and increase in dramatization recorded in the following documents will be noted.

2. *Sacramentary of Angouleme* — most ancient MS of the Carolingian reform (8th-9th Century)

The directives for the dedication of a new church as found in the ritual are as follows:

'The clergy assembles in front of the new church and then enters through the main door. A litany is begun while all are entering the building. At its completion, the bishop takes the water which was m- ixed with wine and blesses them and the whole building. At this time the church furnishing: cross, candles and relics are to remain outside the building until it has been blessed. After the blessing, the clergy approach the altar and another litany is begun. Upon its completion, the celebrant sprinkles the altar, then he anoints the altar with Chrism in the center and at the spot where the relics will be deposited. After anointing sections of the Church building, he blesses the altar linens and chalices, vests the altar, adjusts the altar curtains and lights the candles. All leave the church now and fetch the relics that are awaiting a triumphant entry into the church. The litany accompanies the entry of the relics, which are placed in the altar. Mass is then celebrated.'[97]

It is not difficult to see the rudimentary rite of blessing in this section.

---

95   PL 69, 18.
96   We read of such processions with relics to the churches prepared for en-shrinement in: St. Ambrose's Letter XXII to his sister, PL 16, 1066; St. Augustine's *Confessions* Book IX, Ch. VII; St. Augustine's *City of God*, Book XXII, Ch. VIII.
97   L. Duchesne. *Christian Worship*, pp. 485-486, author's translation.

What is also noticeable is the emergence of a format and plan, yet it remains quite unadorned.

3. *The Roman Ordines from the Manuscript of St. Armand* (c. 800 A.D.) transcribed from an original text.

This document reveals a deeper concern for the relics and the ceremony that surrounds them rather than the celebration and ritual of a church dedication.

'After the singers chant the antiphon and psalm, the bishop goes to the place where the relics are ready, he places them on a tray on which a linen cloth was spread, and covers them vtith a silk cloth. The first prayer is recited by the bishop while a deacon on each side of him supports his arms which are holding the tray. The procession proceeds to the church, amid fragrance of incense and singing of a psalm. (There is a directive that another psalm is to be added if the distance to the church is not yet reached.)

Upon arriving at the Church, the bishop entrusts the relics to the priests, who at this time remain outside the church, they remain there during the litany, together, with the candles and thuribles.

The bishop alone enters the church, sprinkles it with holy water and washes the altar with a sponge. He goes to the church entrance to recite a prayer over the people, who were just sprinkled with what remained of the holy water.

Soon the church doors are opened and the people (universus populus) enter. Once the faithful are present, a psalm is sung while the bishop removes his outer vestment and proceeds by himself to the altar upon which he places the relics to the accompaniment of a text: 'Sub altare Domini sedes accepistis.'

He then closes the areas in which the relics were placed, and begins to anoint the corners of the altar, reciting a prayer to which all present respond: 'Amen'.

The altar is then covered, the bishop puts on his outer vestment and recites another prayer. The altar is adorned with its cloths, candles and cross. The bishop then proceeds to the exterior section of the nave (perhaps the vestry) where the custodian with a lighted candle awaits him, and seeks a blessing from him with the words: 'Sir please, your blessing.' The bishop blesses the flame while praying the words: 'May the Lord, light his house forever.' All present respond: 'Amen'. All the church lights are illuminated, the antiphon begins and the bishop enters the main aisle of the church for the Mass celebration.'[98]

It is easy to interpret this rite as an entombment for the martyr. The emphasis are on the preparation of the altar as a tomb, rather than the dedication of the building in which the faithful, the Church, will assemble to worship. The idea of a majestic burial is further fortified by the use of fragrant oil in the anointing of the altar and the aromatic clouds of incense filling the sanctuary and nave of the church.

One is aware of the fact that the celebrant has a major role to play certain actions call for his performance alone, with or without specific attire, performed to a sung or recited text. The people's response maintains the liaison between the primary and secondary actors and audience, as it were. There seems to be an added ceremony: the bishop approached with a lighted candle at the vestry. The subsequent lighting of all the church candles for the celebration of Mass must have had a dramatic appeal and emotional overtone for all the worshipers. It is evident that further developments and additions occurred.

4. *Sancramentary of Drogo, Bishop of Metz* — 826-855 A.D.

As the son of Charlemagne and Regina, Drogo must have had a desire for beautifying the liturgy as his father had. This sacramentary compiled during his episcopate is copied from a Gregorian examplar, with many Gallican additions. The rite begins at the other chapel where the relics have been kept from the night before.

'...Then the celebrant blesses the water mixed with Chrism with these words... The prayer *Aufer a nobis*[99] is said at the lifting up of the relics

---

[98] Op. cit., pp. 478-479, author's translation.
[99] 'Take away from us our iniquities we ask you, O Lord, that we may be

91

which are now carried to the new church on the bier by the priests. Arriving at the east entrance of the church, the celebrant says a prayer. He then sprinkles the new building and all present with holy water while Psalm 51 is sung.[100] The celebrant then encircles the church three times, knocking at the door and saying each time as he does so: 'Lift up, o gates, your lintels, reach up, you ancient portals that the king of glory may come in! A voice from within the church is heard asking: 'Who is the king of glory?' Finally, at the third time the celebrant responds: 'The Lord, strong and mighty...the Lord of hosts; he is the king of glory'. (Psalm 24)

Then the church doors are opened wide during the singing of the antiphon: 'Walk in O saints of God, enter His House'. Psalm 122 is sung as well.

Then he who previously was inside the church, dashes out of the church, takes his place with the others, only to reenter the church, this time vested in clerical garb. When the celebrant enters the church he says a prayer asking God's blessing on all present.

He then proceeds to sprinkle the interior of the church reciting a prayer.

During the litany, the celebrant and ministers prepare the relics for their place on the altar. The stone that covers the relics is then anointed, together with the four angles of the altar slab. The altar linens and vessels are blessed at this time. The altar is draped (velatur) and Mass begins.[101]

This veil must have been suspended from the rods holding it in place around the baldaquin, which enhanced the altar.[102] More prayers are added to the ritual, as well as the use of Scriptural texts. It is evident that the section of the ritual calls out 'Who is this king of glory?' adds much effect and lays open an area for future development. The cleric, who runs out of the church and then reenters it in ceremonial vestments, seems to be playing two roles, each with

worthy to enter in to the holy of holies with pure minds.'
[100]   Psalm 51:9 is appropriate: 'Cleanse me with hyssop...wash me...'
[101]   L. Duchesne, op. cit., pp. 487-89 author's translation.
[102]   A. Croegaert, *The Mass*, pp. 6-8.

a distinctive costume. There is certainly a thrust toward a dramatic expression on the part of the clergy as well as laity. As long as an action was anchored in a religious text, it would be considered legitimate and appropriate. Within years, a more elaborate ritual would be arrived at. Attention was given to the dedication rituals of Rome and France.

Now one's attention will be turned to Anglo-Saxon England in order to see how the dedication rites were performed in that area of the Empire. Information for our purpose is found in a work attributed to Egbert of York, who was bishop there from 732-766 A.D. Interestingly enough, he was one of Bede's former pupils at Jarrow, and was the founder of the great school at York in which Alcuin was later to be educated.

5. *Pontifical of Egbert of York* — 732-766 A.D.

Although this Pontifical is of the tenth-century, nevertheless it serves our purpose in a literary way for it records the development of a simple stage of dedication to one more elaborate and dramatic.[103] Many features will be most interesting for the reader. There is a sort of Prologue — the announcing on the day on which a certain church would be dedicated. It reads:

'...Dear brothers we request your presence on that day, in that place in which the church will be dedicated in memory of the martyr...do not deny us your presence.

The bishop sees to it that the relics are properly venerated in a befitting place till the next day. During the time, the faithful may pray and keep vigil.

Procedure (Ordo) how a church ought be dedicated. The celebrant and clergy are to vest as they do for Mass. At their arrival at the main entrance of the new church, twelve candles are lighted and placed outside the building in the circle (circuitum).

---

[103] G. G. Willis, *Further Essays In Early Roman Liturgy* (Alcuin Club, London 1968), p. 229 the author maintains that Egbert's Pontifical is too developed to lie on an eight century document, it may contain some elements which come down from that period. A. Croegaert, *The Mass* (Newman Press, 1955), page 36, contains the same observation.

Prayer: asking God to bless beginning and end of one's work.
Antiphon: Luke 19:5-9 '...Zacchaeus, I mean to stay at your house...'

Litany of the Saints: recited in front of the church building.

When the litany is completed, a deacon walks to the church entrance enters and stands behind the door he has closed. The celebrant approaches the church door and strikes it three times with his staff saying:
'Lift up, O gates your lintels, etc...'

After this familiar scene, the celebrant continues with a prayer that God may dwell in the hearts of the believers.

All now enter the church and greet it with the words:

'Peace to this house and to all those who enter and leave it' then the celebrant reaches the midway up the nave, he prays after the deacon signals for all to kneel: *Flectamus genua* the *Levate* — Let us kneel, let us stand.

As the celebrant approaches the altar, the litany is once more sung, during which time all the ministers prostrate before the altar.

The celebrant then begins to trace the letters of the alphabet crosswise on the floor of the church to the text of Psalm 87.

He proceeds to bless the salt which will be used together with blessed ashes in a water mixture for the blessing. Some wine is added to the water. Then he traces a cross with the finger dipped with this water on the corners of the altar, he then walks around the altar several times sprinkling it accompanied with the sung text of Psalm 51. The walls of the church are blessed with this water. He walks with the choir to the main entrance of the church, and sprinkles the outer walls, coming once again up the nave he traces a huge cross the length and width of the floor, during which time, the antiphons are sung. There is a prayer (preface) sung in the center of the nave, asking God's presence, and help to all who seek Him in this building.

The celebrant goes to the altar and pours at its base the remaining water while the words of Psalm 43 are sung: I will go in to the altar of God, the God of my gladness and joy.'

After using incense, he pours the holy oil on the altar and traces a cross in its center, the words of Jacob[104] are recited as he does so. After the consecration of the altar, the celebrant blesses linens and other items which will be used in the sanctuary.

Now the ministers approacr the place where the relics have been prepared for their transferral to the altar. The bier containing them is lifted by the priests, who carry them to the alter amid worthy splendor — clouds of incense and many lighted candles. Once they arrive at the altar, the celebrant parts the curtain, which hangs between the baldaquin and the people. (In doing so, the people will be able to view this part of the ceremony without any obstruction.) At the end of the ceremony, there is a threefold blessing for all present: O Lord, hear me, from your abode in heaven, look upon your flock. Lend them your hand, bless their bodies and souls so that they may receive a heavenly blessing... in the company of the Saints.

May you, O Christ, welcome in your kingdom these who were baptized, who shared your precious Body and Blood, and who were s-igned with your cross on their foreheads.'[105]

When one reads of all the accretions and additions found in the ceremony, one is left with the impression that there was a fusion of two existing rites. Such a conclusion is correct. It was the combination of these two rituals which enhanced the ceremony, making it elaborate and repetitive at times, but nonetheless, it rendered the whole dedication ceremony with an air of drama. The set prayers serve as the dialogue actors normally use, while the various vestments indicate the importance of the servers and their role in the ceremony. The various sections of the ritual with their allotted prayers and action would certainly resemble a scene of a play. For instance, the preparatory ceremony to the Mass can be considered one drama. The sections (scenes) may be summarized as follows:

---

[104]   Genesis 28:16-18.
[105]   Surtees Society Publications, Vol. 27 (Blackwood and Sons, Edinburgh, 1853), pp. 26-52, author's translation.

1. Preparatory Ceremonies — The bishop enters the church, while a litany is chanted.
2. The water for blessings is prepared; the altar is signed with crosses and blessed, then the church walls as well as pavement are sprinkled.
3. The altar itself is consecrated with incense and chrism.
4. Linens, ornaments and other vessels are blessed.
5. The fetching of the relics and their solemn entry into the church.
6. The altar is prepared and dressed for the Mass celebration.

One must remember that the musical accompaniment during the ceremony gave the role very similar to the one given them by the ancient playwrights.

It was during the church dedication that the people had a more active role singing, changing places, and beholding the whole spectacle. Moreover, the section of the ritual which calls for the tracing of Greek and Latin alphabets on the church pavement in cross fashion impresses on the minds of the faithful the impression of a large sign of Christ (X the first letter in the Greek word for Christ), for henceforth this building will be the holy place for worshipers.

d. *Ceremony of the Alphabet*

As soon as the celebrant enters the church, he goes to the eastern corners of the left-hand side of the church and traces the Latin alphabet with the foot of his crozier in the ashes placed there for the purpose. He then repeats the ceremony in another diagonal line across the ash strewn pavement forming a large St. Andrew cross, or again forming the first letter of Christ in Greek. This time, the Greek letters are traced.

Altar

Door

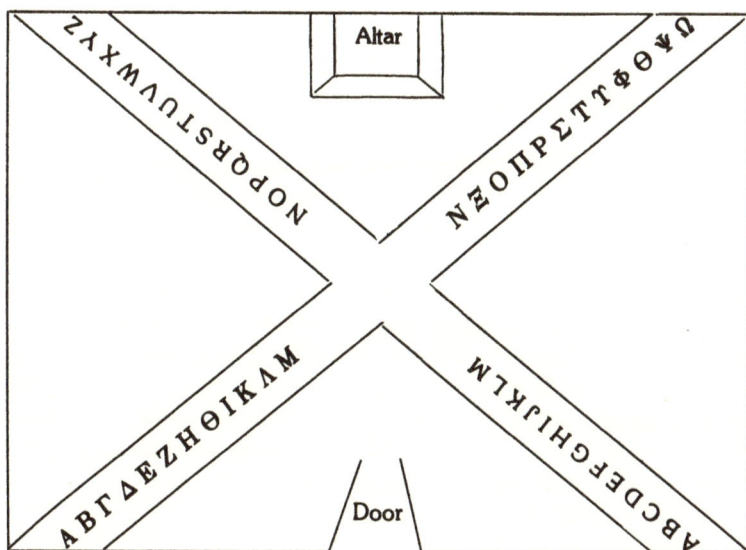

No doubt this ancient custom goes back to a time when Roman surveyors took possession of a piece of property and set its boundaries. Regardless what its historical origin may be, the ceremony of the alphabet certainly contains latent seeds of drama.

It would be safe to view the whole dedication ceremony as a drama in which the elements of tragedy and comedy are present. At its very inception, the mood is that of a funeral; the tomb of a saint is prepared, the triumphant pitch. The chanting of antiphons, psalms and litanies adds much mysticism. The tomb is finally sealed and anointed amid the elaborate ritual of fragrant oil and incense. The climax is reached at the moment the celebrant enters the sanctuary vested for the Mass itself, for now the entire building is claimed for Christ, and He lives among His people. This part of the ritual views the Church as a living person, who is reborn in the waters of baptism and anointed as a living person is at Confirmation. Now the nature of the whole drama is understood, the Church is the symbol of the eternal city, the new Jerusalem, here the bride of Christ (the faithful) anticipate the glimpse of the groom (Christ). By symbol and sacrament the gamos has taken place — the drama that initially set out as a tragedy, finally rests on a note of comedy. The text from Revelation 21:2-3

'I saw a new Jerusalem, the holy city, coming down out of heaven from God, beautiful as a bride prepared to meet her husband…a loud voice from the throne cries out: This is God's dwelling among men, He shall dwell with them…'

carries this sentiment and depicts the nuptial. This anticipation of the union of the lover with the Groom is echoed throughout the dedication rite itself. In Psalm 84, one notices the traits that the Romantics called the 'mal du siecle' or the 'Weltschmerz', the Middle Age monks were to call it 'acedia'. The desire of the believer to be physically present in the temple is found in Psalm 138, while Psalm 96:9 calls for the believer to enter the temple area wearing holy attire! The Christian will always remember that no matter how huge these beautiful buildings be, they will never satisfy the Christians ultimate longing. Seen in perspective, the reader can easily appreciate the position taken by Victor Hugo, by making *the* Cathedral the main character in his novel, as though the Cathedral were alive, and rightly so!

E. *Eyewitness to Church Dedication Ceremonies* — Reveal Dramatic Effect

1. *Ivo of Chartres*, 1040 - Dec. 23, 1115 A.D.

When Ivo of Chartres spoke at a church dedication, he pointed out in detail the symbolism between the ceremonies surrounding the dedication of the building itself, and their similarities in the actual baptism and anointing of a believer. What he left for us was a description of the dedication rite in conjunction with his didactic approach. For our purposes, the emphasis will be on several selections from the rites of dedication.

Speaking of the holy water used in the dedication rite, Ivo says that the use of this water contains the element of penance, while the salt blended with the water symbolizes the teaching of the Gospel. Since the church building cannot be immersed into the baptismal font, its trifold sprinkling with holy water ensures salvation and removal of faults through word and action.

Ivo interprets the rite of the lighting of twelve candles in the empty church as the heritage and teaching of the twelve apostles which has been handed down by the Church to the present day.

When speaking of the celebrant using his staff to knock at the door, three times, Ivo mentions that the people and the clergy enter the church with him. This phase of the ceremony symbolizes the defeat of the evil one. It is as though the question 'Who is this King of Glory' were asked by the people; to which the celebrant exhorts them to open their heavenly doors, that is, their virtues, their doors to a virtuous, holy life. As a result, the doors of death and evil are barred shut.

Ivo mentions the opening of three church doors rather than the main church door. Three doors are symbols of the baptismal grace, teaching of the Word, and the honor conferred on the believer at Confirmation.

When the celebrant enters the threshold with clergy and people, he, together with clergy and people, all greet the building with a trifold 'Peace to this house'.

Ivo continues: when the four corners of the altar are traced with holy water the four corners of the earth are precious to God. This notion is brought to mind when this verse is read from Genesis 28:14:

"...and through them you shall spread out east and west, north and south...all the nations of the earth shall find blessing..."

The words of Psalm 68 and Psalm 91 are very appropriate for chanting during the rite of the sprinkling of the interior walls with holy water. The following words would hear evidence to the reason why this specific psalm was used.

Psalm 68: 6   The father of orphans...is God in his holy dwelling...

17   ...at the mountain God has chosen for his throne, where the Lord himself will dwell forever...

19   ...the Lord enters his dwelling.

25   They view your progress, O God...into the sanctuary.

26   The singers lead, the minstrels follow, in their midst the maidens play on timbrels.

36   Awesome in his sanctuary is God..."

There is very little wonder why Ivo judges these psalms to be appropriate for the ceremony. Psalm 91 was also sung during the ceremony, and precisely because of the text.

Psalm 91: 1   "You who dwell in the shelter of the Most High, who abide in the shadow of the almighty."

It is well observed that even though Ivo gives a symbolic interpretation for the various stages of the dedication rites, he nevertheless uses scriptural texts to justify his interpretation.

This procedure is quite evident at the rite for hallowing the altar. The burning of incense on the altar at this specific moment, symbolizes the prayers of those in heaven. The source for this comment is found in Revelation 8:3-5.

> "Another angel came in holding a censer of gold. He took his place at the altar of incense and was given large amounts of incense to deposit on the altar...from the angels hand the smoke of the incense went up before God and with it the prayers of God's people."

A similar situation exists during the rite for the anointing of the altar, for its being anointed with chrism ensures the presence of the Holy Spirit. The words of Psalm 45, an Epithalamion in praise of the Messianic Kings, reads in verse 3:

> "grace is poured out upon your lips..."

Ivo points out that the rite of putting new linens on the altar calls for the use of Psalm 30, and no wonder; one reads in verse 12:

> "you took off my sackcloth and clothed me with gladness."

In conclusion, Ivo states that his reason for this type of explanation lies with the hope that his hearers may apply themselves to that task which lies ahead, so that what they hear, and what they believe in may all work toward a fruitful completion, with the assurance that the Lord will grant them that needed grace for their renewed undertaking of living a holy life.[106]

Without a doubt, the dedication rites were not only a religious experience for Ivo, but they were also a spectacle in the true sense.

---

[106]   PL 162:531, Sermon IV.

2. *Abbot Suger of St. Denis — 1144 A.D.*

The Abbot of St. Denis set out to build the Abbey Church after searching for able painters, masons and stained glass makers. The result of his keen supervision was the first great Gothic building. One must agree that the possibilities of achieving such a structure were realized at the start in that part of France.[107]

The Abbot mentions the names of various bishops who were present at the consecration and relic translation ceremonies. His detailed account informs us that bishops assembled at the church in the early morning of the day of consecration, their places were in the upper section in the choir, i.e. near the main altar. There they were with their splendidly arrayed vestments, and majestically held their crosiers during the rites.

So great was the attendance of the laity, that one is not surprised to read of the restlessness of those left outside, by the mentioning of their being held back with sticks and poles. In the meantime, the clergy formed the procession leading to the main altar, in which the relics would be placed. A marvel to see! (Mirabile visu!) Those in the procession walked with candles, crosses and other ornament of a festive tone while singing psalms and hymns. After the consecration of the altar, those bishops who were invited, celebrated Mass in the two levels of the building, this solemn and harmonious celebration, delightful and joyful, seemed to be a heavenly symphony rather than a human assembly. It was during this celebration that God joined the timelessness with the material...the wedding of the Eternal Bridegroom.[108]

---

[107] Frederick B. Artz, *The Mind of the Middle Age*, (Alfred Knopf, New York, 1959), p. 390.
[108] PL 186, 1246 from his *Libellus*.

VII
Coronation of Rulers and of Those in Authority

Christianity accepted the social structure of the Middle Ages. The church sanctioned those structures which could be modified and retained as expressions of religious convictions. The coronation of a ruler, in a religious setting, established a relationship between the church and state. The friction and its causes that existed between the two powers will not be included in the scope of this work. Rather, what will be presented to the reader is the fact that the importance of the Coronation Rite called for the ruler to be a holy and just sovereign as an individual combined with lay *and* clerical characteristics — this demanded the loyalty of the subjects. The reality of this situation was exemplified in the dramatic impulses which were channeled and directed in the rite itself. The fact that the rite, with its religious nuances afforded an opportunity for the strata of that society to express this religious experience in a very dutiful and dramatic way.

A. *Early Testimony*

One reads of the early expressions of the newly elected rulers in Tacitus, *Annals* (deals with historic deeds from 14-68 A.D) The practice of hoisting the ruler on a shield was a Germanic expression of assuming rule.

Eusebius mentions the rule of Constantine but doesn't mention the ceremony surrounding his affirming the position as ruler. [109]

The words of the *Euchologium,* 795 A.D., reveal a prayer that asks for God's blessing on the new ruler. A long life, just rule and strength are prayed for so that the ruler may be an heir of heaven. The people cry out three times: "Holy, holy, holy! Glory to God in the heavens, and peace on earth!" [110] These instances could hardly support the reasons why the Church pursued the rites of coronation with some ceremonies. One must turn to the Sriptures for the text and setting of the coronation rite as found in the Old Testament.

B. Coronation Rites as Recorded in the Old Testament

The reader will find the detailed accounts of an enthronement anointing and homage in 1 Kings 1:32-48 and 2 Kings 11:12-20. It is evident that the rite was divided into two sections: the first part was ceremonially performed in the sanctuary: it was followed by the second phase of the ceremony performed in the palace. The following layout will make for an interesting observation.

1. The Sanctuary

1 Kings 1:39
"Then Zadok the priest took the horn of oil from the tent and anointed Solomon.. all the people shouted: "Long live King Solomon!""

2 Kings 16:18
"In deference to the king...he removed from the temple the emplacement which had been built in the temple for a throne."

---

[109] Eusebius *Church History*, Bk. VIII, Ch. 13 states "being proclaimed supreme emperor and augustus by the soldiers...king of all". One wonders if there was a military shield tossing.

[110] For interesting reading of Eastern Coronations cf. A.E.R. Boak's *Imperial Coronation Ceremonies of the Fifth and Sixth Centuries,* 'Harvard Studies', Vol XXX, Oxford University Press, 1919, pp. 37-47.

This would indicate that there was a place reserved for the king in the Temple, the king would be in this place during the ceremonies of coronation.

2. Investing King with Insignia of New Office

2 Kings 11:12

'Then Jehoiada led out the king's son and put the crown (nezer) and the insignia on him. They proclaimed him king and anointed him, clapping their hands and shouting: "Long live the king."'

Although the Hebrew word for insignia 'eduth' is used, its meanings may include bracelets or protocol. The sceptre, for some unknown reason, had no place in the ceremony. The figure of God as king is clearly presented in Psalm 103:

Psalm 103: 4   he crowns you with kindness and compassion.

19   The Lord has established his throne in heaven, and his kingdom rules over all.

3. The Anointing of the King

1 Samuel 9:16

"...I will send you a man from the land of Benjamin whom you are to anoint as commander of my people.' 1 Samuel 10:1-2 continues this action.

2 Samuel 5:3

"When the elders came to David in Hebron...they anointed him king of Israel."

2 Kings 12:30

"Then the people took Jehoahaz, son of Josiah, anointed him, and proclaimed him king..."

1 Samuel 16:12-13

"David is anointed."

It becomes evident that the rite of anointing was performed in the temple by a priest, hence the ceremony becomes a religious one. The king as the anointed one of God is referred to in Psalms 18:51; 89:39; 132:10. The king is also a consecrated person thereby sharing in God's holiness. This fact is clearly recorded in several texts: 1 Samuel 24:7; 26:9, 23. The reigning king is therefore a messiah; the translation from the Hebrew 'mashiah' — 'the anointed'.

4. Acclamations

1 Kings 1:34
"Then Zadok the priest and Nathan the prophet are to anoint him king of Israel and you shall blow the horn an cry, "Long live King Solomon.""

2 Kings 11:12
"Then...they proclaimed him king and anointed him, clapping their hands and shouting: 'Long live the king.'"

One easily notices the directive to shout at this ceremony. This shouting was not a sign that the choice of king was made by the people; rather it was a sign of approval on the people's part. One must keep in mind the fact that the king was God's choice and as a result the king's authority was a share in God's; it is for this reason that the community gladly submits to it. The people's voices are heard again in 1 Samuel 10:24.

5. The Royal Throne

2 Kings 11:19
"...the guard led the king down from the temple through the guards' gate to the palace where Joash took his seat on the royal throne."

This part of the ceremony took place in the royal palace. To sit on the throne had the same meaning as beginning a reign. The assuming of power by the king must have been very impressive, especially when one reads of the throne he ascended described vividly in 1 Kings 10:18-20.

"The king (Solornon) had a large ivory throne made, and overlaid it with refined gold. The throne had six steps, a back with a round top, and an arm on each side of the seat. Next to each arm stood a lion, and twelve other lions stood on the steps, two to a step, one on either side of each step."

6.   *Homage Paid to the New King*
1 Kings 1:47

"...and the kings servant went in and paid their respects to our lord, King David saying: 'May God make Solomon more famous than you and exalt his throne more than your own!"

In return, the new king would confirm his servants in their offices.

C.   *Dramatic Overtones at Biblical Coronation Rites*

From the above selections, one would gather that these royal coronations were accompanied by popular enthusiasm and participation. The shouting of 'Long live the king!' would attest to that fact, however there was also cheering, flute and trumpet playing together with an air of drama. Among the many songs praising the new ruler, Psalms 2 and 110 set a mood of enthronement. Mention is made of annointing royal investiture, and homage. Psalm 72 offers a prayer that the king may rule justly, and foretells that his rule will extend to the ends of the earth.

Other texts will show how kings of Biblical times performed priestly functions. One reads that Saul offered sacrifice at Gilgal (1 Samuel 13:9-10 David dramatically offered sacrifice at Jerusalem (2 Samuel 6:13, 17-18); for the Temple dedication, Solomon offers sacrifice at Jerusalem (1 Kings 8:5, 62-64). David wears the priestly vestment (2 Samuel 6:14), and blesses the people, a rite reserved to the priests (1 Kings 8:14). It is evident that the royal anointing empowered the king with certain perogatives which made it possible for him to act as the religious leader of the people.[111]

This aspect is clearly presented in Zechariah 6:11-14.

---

[111]   Ronald de Vaux, O.P. *Ancient Israel* (Darton, Longman & Todd, London, 1961), Chapter Five — the Person of the Sing, pp. 100-114.

"Silver and gold you shall take, and make a crown; place it on the head of Zerubbabel...Yes, he shall build the temple of the Lord and taking up the royal insignia, he shall sit as ruler upon his throne."

Most attention is given to David as the king who played well the many roles of his office. The fact that he was a musician, director, major character, and king, is clearly pointed out in Sirach 47:6-10:

"...when he assumed the royal crown he battled... with his every deed he offered thanks to God in words of praise...and daily had His praises sung.

He added beauty to the feasts and solemnized the seasons of each year with string music before the altar, providing sweet melody for the psalms so that when the Holy Name was praised before daybreak the sanctuary would resound."

D. Christian Coronation Ceremony — A Legitimate Source for Dramatic Expression

While the Church was directly opposing the licentious representations of a decadent paganism through dramatic form, it was also indirectly encouraging a dramatic representation of scriptural beliefs. Royal coronations, for instance, sought their rudimentary elements from the pages of the Scriptures, while they received the sanction of the religious leader (bishop or pope). The fact that they were publicly witnessed, allowed for some popular involvement and dramatic channeling. This soon-religious rite was to grow and develop through many stages, that it became a contributing factor which kept alive a dramatic desire in he people of Early Medieval Europe.[112]

The early history of the coronation ceremony as recorded in the West, gives one the impression that the Church transformed the barbaric warrior into a Christian being. A sacred duty was imposed upon this personage, which rendered him laymen, part cleric. It was only natural for the clergy of that

---

[112] The scope of this work will include the western part of Europe. For interesting reading on the subject of coronations in Eastern Europe cf: (A) A.E.R. Boak. *Imperial Coronation Ceremonies of the Fifth and Sixth Centuries,* Harvard Studies in Classical Philosophy, Vol. XXX, Oxford University press, 1949. (B) F.E. Brightman, *Byzantine Imperial Coronations,* The Journal of Theological Studies, Vol. 2, p. 359. (C) Sabine G. MacCormack, *Art and Ceremony in Late Antiquity...*

period, to look back into the Old Testament for paragons who would support that which was performed. In the Scriptures, they found what they were looking for i.e. David's anointing, etc...Adding Scriptural texts to already basic rites, as the Teutonic tribal practice of 'lifting' or 'tossing' the ruler on a shield, the Church rendered the rite more elaborate. The oil used was chrism, the same oil and balsam mixture which was used at Confirmation and Ordinations. No wonder then that the anointing became a very important feature of the coronation rite; it also was regarded as having some sacramental qualities. Indeed, the earliest accounts of kingly coronations are spoken of as ordination, the anointing seems to take preference over any other phase of the whole ceremony. It is evident from the writing of the following witnesses that the anointing was deemed essential to the 'making of a king' and perhaps it was all that was required.

E. *Early Evidence of Anointing and Blessing of Rulers*

1. *St. Gregory, Pope* — 590-604 A.D.

One learns from reading the commentary of Pope Gregory on I Kings X that the kings of his day were anointed. Thus he writes:

> "Ungatur caput regis...the king's head is anointed because his whole being is overflowing with the Divine Physician's spiritual favors and grace."[113]

2. Julian of Toledo

The steps, recorded in Julian's Historia, which precede the actual anointing of the Visigothic kings were the taking of a solemn oath assuring the people royal assistance and protection, this was proclaimed as the king extended his hand on the Gospels. There is no indication that a crown was bestowed on the king, nor is there evidence in the work, that the king received any insignia of his office. By the solemn unction, the king's role was clearly realized and appreciated by all. It is with this in mind that Julian records for us an interesting incident which took place at King Wamba's anointing in 672 A.D.

---

[113] PL 79:278, author's translation.

"The king entered the church of St. Peter and St. Paul, approached the altar, there he pledged support to his subject, as was the custom. Then he knelt (curvatis genibus) for the anointing. It happened, that when bishop Quiricius anointed his head, a cloud of smoke or vapor arose from the very spot which had been amply anointed with Chrism; this vapor in the shape of a dove, presently rested upon the king's head. All those present saw this marvel and considered it as a token of divine approval."[114]

Here one reads of the bare essential element around which the other rites would later be joined to construct a more elaborate ceremony. Already, one sees the king as the principle character, the clergy as secondary characters and the people — the audience.

3. *Charlemagne* — Chrismas Day, 800 A.D.
    Frankish King — Roman Emperor

On that Christmas Day, Charlemagne and his son enter the Basilica of St. Peter. Before the Mass itself, Charlemagne prays before the Confession of St. Peter. When he rose to his feet, Pope Leo III placed a crown on his head. The Basilica was filled with many people who shouted in unison at this point: "Life and victory to Charles Augustus, crowned by God. The mighty and peaceful emperor!"[115] There is no mention of a Germanic custom of 'lifting' or 'hoisting' the ruler on a shield. The elected emperor would have been raised on a shield and carried around the camp three times.

Although this dramatic gesture was never performed at Charlemagne's Coronation, there is mention of yet another dramatic feature — the *Laudes*. These Royal *Laudes* must have been composed considerably early, perhaps in Pepin's time and certainly by 774 A.D., since in that year Pope Hadrian had them sung for Charlemagne during his stay in Rome. The format is clearly the style used for emperor-worship of pagan Rome and Christianized in form to the Byzantine liturgy.

It begins: Christ is Victor, Christ Reigns, Christ Rules.

---

[114] PL 96:766, author's translation.

[115] L. Duchesne. *Liber pontificalis,* Vol. II. p. 6, DeBoccard, Paris, 1955. PL 102:1003A.

109

Hear us, O Christ	Long life to Leo, supreme pope and universal Pontiff.
Savior of the World	help him
St. Peter	help him
Hear us, O Christ	Long life and victory to Charles, the most excellent crowned by God, peaceful king of the Franks and Lombards, and patrician of the Romans...
Redeemer of the World	help him.
St. Mary...	help him.
St. Stephen...	help him.
Hear us, O Christ	Long life to the most noble royal family.
Holy Virgin of Virgins	help them.
St. Silvester	help them.
Hear us, O Christ	Long life and victory to all the judges and whole army of the Franks.
St. Hilary	help them.
St. Denis...	help them.

Christ is Victor, Christ Reigns, Christ Rules

King of Kings	Christ is Victor
Our king...	Christ is Victor
Our Victory	Christ is Victor

To him alone honor, glory, and praise through endless years, for ever and ever. Amen.

Kyrie Eleison	Lord have mercy, (three times).
Happiness	

May your time be good
May your years be many. Amen

To appreciate the dramatic effect this rite contained, one has to be reminded that the words were sung to simple yet majestic melodies. One clearly sees there invocations are followed by a series of acclamations addressed to the Triumphant Christ, protector of the Franks. Finally, new appeals to Christ and hopes for happiness, prosperous times and long life are addressed with firm confidence Here one sees good wishes and shouts of happiness for the new king who is now elevated above all his subjects. An awesome message and dramatically presented! The the Pope anointed Charles with holy oil, and likewise anointed his son (...unxit oleo sancto Karol filio eius, rege, in ipso die Natalis..)[116] It would suffice to demonstrate the simple yet majestic rite of 'blessing' Charlemagne as emperor.

The Crowning	this action performed by the pope as major character, he himself places the crown on the sovereign's head.
The Acclamations	the people's shouts for joy, sung as refrain, expressing
Laudes	their part in the whole affair. No doubt the pope's nod signaled this chorus simply drama.
The Anointing	the pope anoints Charles with chrism.

The one positive feature of this account of Charlemagne's coronation is the mention of the Acclamations. One must remember that the faithful in that part of the empire were no longer finding Latin as understandable as their forefathers, now the vernaculars were appearing. It is during this period that the negative feature of the Church's liturgy become more and more foreign to the worshiping community. This shouting of the *Laudes* would seem to them as a last straw they could hold on to, the only expression of worship, which although in Latin was at least understood, in the ocean of clerical Latin.

4. *Hincmar of Rheims* — 806-889 A.D.

During the Carolingian Era, this bishop of Rheims had influenced the

---

[116]   Op. cit. p. 7. (Liber pontificales, Puchesne, p. 7.) Musical notation for the Laudes may be obtained in the St. Gregory Hymnal.

Frankish kingdom by his legal and theological writings. One aspect has been often neglected — his composition of the coronation rites for Queen Judith, and King Charles the Bald.

a) Coronation of Judith, Charlemagne's Daughter. 856 A.D.

When Judith married the English king, Edelulfus, the ceremony seems to have combined the elements of a wedding and a coronation. Surprisingly one becomes aware of the orderly wording, ritual and dramatic crescendo. The rite is as follows:

Blessing on the Queen

> "May you marry in Christ, undertake this union with your eyes open, ever alert, shun your eyes from vanity, say with the Psalmist; 'I lifted my eyes up to the mountain...'"

> 'Lord, bless this dowry (dotes) may she merit fellowship with your saints..."

The ring is presented with these words:

> "Receive this ring, as a sign of faith and love, may it also symbolize this union; man may not separate what God joins together."

The rite continues with words of encouragement:

> "I promise you to one man, be a true spouse to your husband as the women we read about in the Scriptures — Sara, Rebecca, Rachel, Esther, Naomi, etc..."

> "Lord, shower your blessings on the couple...may they grow in mutual holiness. Open for the heaven's doors and visit them in peace. May their lands be productive so as to produce spiritual fruits. Grant them salvation and bid them enter your kingdom.

Blessing of the Queen

Lord, we ask you that your servant who you deemed grow in the happy flower of youth, may grow day by day in virtue and be made worthy to live in peace.

So far, no mention is made of the role of queenship, etc... It is at the preface of the Mass that one hears of the coronation theme: the queen's name is mentioned, together with the anointing of Aaron and David. The preface continues to recount how Judith of old was chosen by God to free her peoples, and set the enemies in confusion. Now may her heart be filled with peace and simplicity. Finally, the *Crowning* itself is accompanied with these words:

May the Lord crown you with glory and honor and place on your head a crown of precious spiritual gems, so that your good acts and deeds may reflect your virtues as the shining gems reflect their brilliance.

One notices that the emphasis is laid upon the request to live a virtuous life rather than to rule wisely. Nevertheless, this information affords us with the basic element of dramatically representing a union of two roles for the bride — the role of a wife and the role of a queen. The rite concluded with a blessing specially directed toward her.

Final Blessings

Lord, we ask you, bless your servant...	Amen
Lord, receive the work of her hands...	Amen
May blessings be always yours in abundance...	Amen
May she be blessed with a family as was Abraham...	Amen

b) Coronation of Charles the Bald
869 A.D.[117]

Without doubt, the selection Hincmar wrote for this coronation ceremony, reveals to us a very elaborate and dramatic peak in the evolution of royal coronations. The different prayers assigned to the various visiting bishops seem to indicate the role of actors played with their specific lines. The

---

[117]   PL 125:811.

progression of the rite entails a dramatic climax, while the presentation of royal insignia echoes the idea of costume and wardrobe.

The Rite

Before the Mass, the king approaches the altar, and there receives the blessing from visitng bishop.

Bishop of Metz	Lord, grant wisdom to your servant, may he be totally dedicated to you and your teachings.
Hatto of Verdun	Lord may he pursue your law and abide in your commands....
Arnulfus of Toul	Lord may his rule secure us your peace, so be kind to him......
Franco of Tongres	Lord, give your servant health of mind and body, may he continue to do good, and respect your law....
Hincmar of Mount Loon	Lord may this your servant receive your blessing, and always render you thanks, may he always find favor before you.
Odo of Beauvais	Lord, preserve your servant, fill him with your gift, purify him and make him fruitful in doing your will....
Hincmar	May the Lord open his right hand. May the Lord's mercy flow upon you. May the Lord's protection be a happy defense around you (filici muro) through the prayers of Mary and all the saints.

At this point the directive reads:
Hincmar, the bishop, anoints him with chrism at the right ear, on the forehead to the left ear, and on the head....with these words:

May the Lord crown you with the crown of glory in his mercy; and may He anoint you with the oil of the Holy Spirit's favor, with which the priest, prophets and kings were anointed....Amen.

It continues:

May you be victorious over all foes visible and invisible.   Amen.
Happiness be yours and your people's.   Amen.

May you rule over your people happily, with love during your reign.   Amen

Now the actual coronation is performed by the bishops, using these words they place the crown on the sovereign's head:

May the Lord crown you with glory and justice...so with a deep faith you may attain the crown of glory.

At this point, the king is bestowed the insignia, with these words:

May the Lord give you the will and power to accomplish His will and attain eternal glory with the palm of perseverance. Amen.

After he is presented with the royal sceptre and palm, the ceremony continues with the continuation of the Mass.[118]

It is quite evident that Charles the Bald was crowned on the head alone, and there only in three places: the right ear, the forehead round to the left ear, and then on the crown of the head.

The whole ceremony speaks of a dramatic presentation; the seven bishops, each saying a prayer, seems to indicate his role as supporting actors reciting his specific lines in a play. One can easily visualize this ceremony as a highly dramatic and spectacular work which achieves the level of dramatic expression of the people's faith and belief.

There is an added feature to the coronation of Louis II.

5.   Louis II — 887 A.D.

Petition of Bishops	We seek your pardon... according to counciliar decrees, etc...
King's Promise	According to his royal position he grants pardon, canonical privilegest legal debts and promise to perceive justice as a king ought to act.
Blessing over the King	Grant him a spirit of wisdom so he may be totally devoted to you, the church and all, may he remain in your peace.

---

[118]   PL 125:803, author's translation.

Anointing (Infusio) with holy oil	the prayer used refers to Joshua, David, Saul and Solomon...may this anointing reach his inner being and may he live up to his promises.
Crowning	Crown him, Lord, with justice, glory, honor and strong deeds.
Handing of Scepter	Receive this sign of rule, this staff of virtue...may you rule well and wisely. May you set wrongs aright, correct evils...may God assist you in all you do...Amen.
Blessing — Based on Numbers 6:23-27	May the Lord shine His face on you and give you His peace. Amen. May He grant you favor, pardon and mercy. Amen. May you be victorious over enemies. May He lead you to eternal happiness in His kingdom wearing the crown of victory.[119]

The beginning of this ceremony seems to be presented as a dialogue. The anointing, crowning and vestiture with the scepter seems to deserve full attention. The other rites lean toward text and action for support. All attest to a dramatic effect which pervades the whole ceremony.

F.*Anglo-Saxon England*

The medieval period was mainly a religious age, in which faith and liturgy permeated most customs and other social activities. It would be only natural, therefore, for the political and social realms to share in the transcendent quality of that belief. The Old Testament figure, Melchisedech, was the person who united the dignity of king with that of priest in his own person, and this fact resulted in the church's unique approach toward monarchs. The anointing with chrism was a rite used in priestly ordinations as well as in kingly coronations. It remains obvious why the faithful treated the monarch with respect, as being a representative of legitimate authority as well as a person to be held in high religious esteem. This belief was brought out in dramatic details during the coronation rite itself. During the centuries, the coronation rite developed from a rudimentary 'blessing' to a more elaborate ceremony very similar to the ordination ceremonies reserved by the Church for its bishops and priests.

There seems to have been a clever balance between the text and

---

[119]   PL 125; 809-811, author's translation.

dramatization developed at this time in England. This aspect of inner belief expressed through external prayer is clearly grasped when considering the coronation of King Edgar.

1) *King Edgar* — 973 A.D.

Edgar and his wife were crowned at St. Peter's, Bath on Pentecost, May 11, 973; the ceremony was performed by Dunstan and St. Oswald, archbishops. The various steps of the ceremony are very intricate and would seem to give the impression of one act having many scenes. Although this liturgical setting emphasizes the spiritual side of the ceremony, the element of drama cannot be overlooked!

Components of the Rite

Entrance	The king, robed and crowned is led by two bishops into the church. As he approaches the altar, he removes his crown; while the choir sings the *Te Deum*, he prostrates himself.
Oath	When the *Te Deum* is completed, the bishops raise the king and he gives his promise to rule his realm justly. All attention was on the king as he swore: Peace for all his people; establish law and order; his reassurance of being just and merciful in meting out justice. All present answered: Amen.
Prayers	Invocations were uttered to God to send down His blessings on His servant...asking God to grant him the faith of Abraham, the gentleness of Moses, the strength of Joshua, the humility of David, the wisdom of Solomon, and to help him nourish, strengthen and build God's people committed to him. After the prayers came the Antiphon: 'And Zadok, the priest, and Nathan, the prophet, anointed Solomon, King in Sion', and approaching the king they exclaimed:
Anointing and Acclamation	'May the King live for ever!' Vivat rex in aeternum. It was during the antiphon that the king was anointed. Here we have the heart of the ceremony — the climax of a play, as it were.

117

Investiture *Conferring* *Regalia*	After appropriate prayers, the sword was presented to the king. The crown was now placed on his head, to the words..."preserve him in health, prosperity and happiness...protect and defend him." The scepter was presented to him at this point. After presenting the king with the Rod of justice, the blessing was prayed by the prelate:
Blessing	References of the Old Testament seem to abound: "so glorify him, Lord...that he may hold the scepter of Solomon, with the sublimity of David...as you permitted Solomon to obtain a peaceful kingdom". When all the prayers were completed, the king was addressed with words defining his royal position, an Epilogue at the end of a play.
Meaning of Being *a Christian King*	'Stand and grasp your royal position now...delegated by God...May he make you reign with him in His eternal kingdom.

The queen was then anointed and the Mass continued.[120]

2) Egbert's Pontifical

One reads of similar dramatic overtones in the Pontifical of Egbert of York, 732-767 A.D. It is no wonder that early drama developed and flourished as it did in England with such a rich liturgical heritage to channel the already existing dramatic impulse. The reliance on scriptural text is quite evident in the work of Egbert:

Mass for kings on the day of blessing

Antiphon: Psalm 119-137	'You are just, O Lord and your ordinance is right'
Psalm: Psalm 119:1	'Happy are they whose way is blameless, who walk in the law of the lord.'

---

[120] PL 159:798; Brooke, Christopher, *The Saxon and Norman Kings*, Fontana Press, England, 1972; Godfrey, John, *The Church in Anglo-Saxon England*, Cambridge University Press, England, 1972.

Prayer:	'O Lord, you are the protector of all kingdoms and Christian rule, grant to your servant our king, the triumnphant of his virtues...'
Reading: Leviticus 26:6,9	'I will establish peace in the land, that you may lie down to rest without anxiety...'
Gradual: Psalm 29:7	'The Lord has given victory to his anointed...'
Gospel: Matthew 27:15	'...which one do you wish me to release to you, Barabbas or Jesus the socalled Messiah?'

Then follows the *Blessing* upon the newly elected king:

Prayer:	after this prayer, the horn of oil is poured open upon the king's head, while one bishop says the prayer, the other bishops anoint him.
Investiture with scepter:	after the anointing, the bishops with the princes give the scepter to the king.
Prayers:	These consist of fifteen short pleas with the popular Amen.

...May he always fear you Lord, may he fight for you, may he be a shield in a peaceful kingdom...   Amen.
...Grant him favor all his day, Lord, and may his reign be full of justice...   Amen
...Be for him, Lord, honor, joy and solace in times of trouble, council in time of doubt and comfort in life's journey.   Amen.
etc...

The staff is then presented to the king; the prayer recited, asking for the blessing of Abraham, Isaac, and Jacob.

Now the bishops take the crown and place it on the king's head. After the prayer, all present are directed to shout in unison, three times: 'Vivat rex N. In sempeternum!' 'May king N. live for ever!' Amen. Amen. Amen.

After another prayer over the king, the Mass continues as usual.[121]

D.   *Continental Witness*

1.   *Aachen* — 936 A.D.

Less elaborate but equally interesting in it dramatic scope is the scene at the Coronation of Otto I in 936.

> ...and when all were assembled there, the dukes and the commanders of the soldiers and other military leaders raised Otto upon the throne, which was erected in the portico adjoining the church of Charlemagne, ...they made him king according to their custom.
>
> Meanwhile the archbishop of Mainz and the clergy and people awaited him within the church. When he finally approached, the archbishops met him and went with him to the center of the church; then turning to the people...he said: 'I bring you Otto,...if this choice pleases you, raise your right hands.' At this, the whole people raised their right hands to heaven and hailed the new ruler with a mighty shout.
>
> Then the archbishop advanced with the king, who was clothed with a short tunic after the Frankish custom, to the altar, on which lay the royal insignia, the sword and belt, the cloak and armlets, the staff with the scepter and diadem.
>
> The archbishop, going up to the altar, took up the sword and belt and turning to the king, said: 'Receive this sword with which you shall cast out all the enemies of Christ...'
>
> Then taking up the cloak and armlets he put them on the king and said: 'The borders of this cloak trailing on the ground shall remind you that you are to be zealous in the faith and to keep peace.'
>
> Taking up the scepter and staff, he said: 'By these symbols you shall

---

[121]   Cf. above footnote, 101.

correct your subjects… may the oil of mercy never be lacking to your head, that you may be crowned here and in the future life with an eternal reward.'

The king is then anointed with the sacred oil and crowned with the golden crown, he is then led to the throne, which he ascended. The throne was built between two marble columns of great beauty and was so placed that the king could be seen by all present.

After the Mass and the singing of the *Te Deum*, the king descended from the throne and entering the palace where a banquet was awaiting them all.[122]

This ceremony indicates the importance which was placed upon the insignia, and the words which accompany this fact clearly point it out. Perhaps, what is striking is the mention of asking the people to raise their hands and shout as a sign of favor at the selection of the sovereign. The position of the throne in the clear sight of all, undoubtedly created a dramatic atmosphere.

It is not a surprise to learn that the elements of liturgy and theology were so interwoven that the whole ceremony seemed as another sacrment. This opinion reached the peak of popularity during the time of St. Peter Damian.

2)   *St. Peter Damian* — 1007-1072 A.D.

Born in northern Italy, Peter became a theologian and reformer as a monk. In his writings, he refers to royal anointings as a sacrament. It is in his description that one reads of the symbolism surrounding the specific actions, all of which enhances the aspect of drama!

'…the candidate (king) is led to the altar. He is vested, then with his own hand he swears to maintain the church's freedom.

His former clothes are put aside, he is then sprinkled (aspergitur) with the holy oil, so that he may be glorified with the fullness of the heavenly anointing. He is then vested in purple robes, which is the sign

---

[122]   Norton Downs, *Medieval Pageant*, D. Van Nostrand Co., New York City, 1964, pp. 83-84.

of royal majesty. The gold crown is placed on his head, expressing holiness, glory and honor and works of virtue.

A sword is set before him so that he becomes aware that he is the vindicator of God's anger.

After he is instated with many such rites, he is led to the palace. From that day forward, he is feared as well as loved.

It would be a happy situation to have the sword of priestly power soften the royal sword, and the royal sword to sharpen the priestly sword. These are the two swords we read about in the Lord's passion, Luke 11:38:

"They said, Lord here are two swords."[123]

Even with the mention of symbolic overtones, this presentation reflects the dramatic outlet of text and gesture and the outcome when these two elements are joined together.

3) Papal Coronations

St. Peter Damian also considered the coronation of the pope as another sacrament. In his describing the various steps of the rite, he has left a portrayal which is rich in dramatic overtones.

Anointing	The pope's head is anointed. His hands are then
Psalm 23:5	anointed, so that he may bless...
Gospel Book	The Book of Gospels is placed open upon his head, so that his words in this life may exceed the mere senses, and his eyes be fixed on proclaiming the Lord's Word eloquently,,,
Insignia	A cidaris, (most likely a mitre) is placed on his head once he is consecrated and a golden sword is presented him, signifying glory.
Psalm 119:112	A ring is given to him to wear on his finger.

---

[123] PL 144:899, author's translation.

| Isaiah 52:7, | His feet are then shod so as to be prepared to preach |
| Ephesians 6:15 | the Gospel of Peace. |

He then grasps his staff gently so that he may rebuke the restless. [124]

Another version is recorded thusly:

"...after the pope ascends his throne, after the *Kyrie* a bishop says the first prayer, followed by another bishop and the second prayer.

The Gospel Book is then opened and held over his head by the assisting deacons.

After this, the subdeacons tie the pallium on him. He then ascends the throne once again and gives the Kiss of Peace to all present, then intones the *Gloria*...' [125]

The above rites reveal the fact that those very ceremonies were supported by Scriptural texts and eventually found their legitimate channelling toward a dramatic realization fostered by the Church's liturgy. How well aware was Shakespeare of the coronation rites and the importance placed on the part of anointing:

'Not all the water in the rough rude sea can wash the balm' off from an anointed king.'

King Richard II, Act III, Sc. 11, 1. 54

Samuel Pepys (1633-1703) records the impression he experienced at the coronation of Charles II, in his diary, April 23, 1661.

---

[124]   PL 144:899, author's translation.
[125]   PL 78:918, author's translation.

VIII
Monastic Influence

The monastery was a little world of its own. The time and stability of those living there (monks) contributed to the shaping and influencing of their liturgical lifestyle. Ceremonies became intricate and time consuming. These ceremonies served as channels by which their own dramatic impulses could be actualized. Next to the celebration of the Mass, the Divine Office played an important part, if not, the sole part of the horarium of the community. The context of the Divine Office included the entire Psalter, which was recited once a week, the entire Old and New Testaments which were read with suitable commentaries once a year; the Church's year began on the first Sunday of Advent.

A.   *Divine Office*

An outline of the Office (Off icium Divinum — Divine Duty) will help elucidate the reason why the Monastic community was so influenced. Matins and Lauds began the day. These long portions (Hours) of the Office were prayed at the early hours of the day, shortly after midnight. There was the:

Introduction:	"Lord open my lips"
Psalm 3:	influenced by verse 6, "I lay down and I sleep, I arose"
Psalm 94:	Invitation to prayer.
	Invitatory — "Come let us exult the Lord...Let us kneel before Him..."
Hymn:	Varied according to feast or solemnity.

Nocturn I:	Six psalms with antiphons — sung antiphonally. Three reading selections from the Scriptures each followed by responsories.
Nocturn II:	Six psalms with alleluia. Brief reading from St. Paul. Versicle and response.
Conclusion:	"Preces" litanies.

On Sundays and major feast days the *Te Deum* was chanted. The Gospel was likewise chanted; after a short commentary read from the Church Fathers, the Abbots blessing was given, after which Laudes would begin with the intent of bringing this hour right to the break of day.

The other hours of the Office were referred to by the time of day at which they were to be prayed.

Prime — Early morning, after Lauds, around 6:00 a.m.

Terce — 9:00 a.m.

Sext — Noon

Nones — 9th hour i.e. around 3:00 p.m.

Vespers — The Evening Prayer, ranks in importance with Matins and Lauds.

Compline — Final prayer recited by community before retiring.

The monastic daily schedule was balanced by prayer and work.

B. *Regularis Concordia* — 980 A.D.

When England was left in disarray after the Viking invasions, King Edgar tried to reorganize monastic life in his realm. The monasteries, one must remember, formed the backbone of learning and culture. It was with this fact in mind that Edgar called a council at Winchester to reestablish a discipline for the monks throughout his realm, thereby bringing order and unity to every area of the kingdom. When all the parties finally agreed in general to certain directives, the task to itemize all the terms was left to St. Ethelwold, hence the name of this document became *Ethenwold's Code* or known often enough as *The Rule Reached by General Agreement*. The obvious presence of many interesting features with dramatic intent included in this work surely makes it the first document dealing with drama on English soil.

125

1) *Purification of Mary* — Candlemas
(cf. Egeria's description above)

This feast commemorates the event in the life of Jesus when His parents presented Him at the Temple. The ceremony calls for the monks to light their candles at the church. They are to recite the psalms while going there. Then the Abbot, vested in stole and cope, shall bless the candles, sprinkle them with holy water and incense them. When the Abbot receives his candle, the chanting of pertinent scriptural texts begin and the monks receive and light their own candles. During the procession they should have sung antiphons describing the feast (text from Luke 2:26-27). Upon reaching the church entrance, the responses indicating the feast are sung. Next, the Lord's prayer was said and Terce followed. The directive is given that the monks should be vested for Mass during which they held their lighted candles until the Offertory, when they were offered to the celebrant.

Again, what is so clear is the presence of dramatic elements of action, actors, script, timing and cues.

2) *Palm Sunday*

Procession	Vested in albs, the monks are to go to the church where the palms are. Upon reaching the church, a prayer is said.
ᴴ𝑥ᵋᵞλ	The section of the text: Turba multa is read by the deacon as far as the words "ecce mundus...."
Blessing of Palms	The palms are to be sprinkled with holy water and then they are incensed.
Distribution	While the children (pueri) are singing the antiphon "The Hebrew Children", the palms are to be distributed. The procession begins toward the main church.
Processions at Main Church	As soon as they arrive, the monks shall wait while the children, walking before them, sing the hymn *Gloria laus*.
Entry into the Church	Upon the completion of the hymn *Gloria laus*, the leader of song intones the responsory: *Ingrediente Domino* — when the Lord entered (Jerusalem), the church doors are opened, all the monks enter, they

hold their palms in their hands until the offertory (dum Offertorium cantetur).

This ceremony reveals a dramatic plot, Scriptural text supplies the rationale for the action which follows. The singing and processing to a specific place intensifies the emotions. One could almost sense the catharsis of the whole rite at the grand entry into the church; this point parallels the whole aspect of commemoration, i.e. Christ's entry into the city of Jerusalem.

3) *Holy Thursday*

The ceremony consisted in the Abbot's washing the feet of all present in his own basin, drying and kissing them while assisted by servers, when he returns to his own seat, where his own feet are washed by the senior monks of the community.

The fact remains quite evident, there is no elaborate or distinctive type liturgy to accompany this rite; the bare essential is retained whereas a more involved ceremony was in use in France and Spain.

4) *Good Friday*

The directives for 'strengthening the faith of the unlearned common persons' (ad fidem indocti vulgi corroborandam) suggest: that on the part of the altar where there is a space for it, there would be a space as a sepulchre, a curtain would hang about it, after the cross was venerated, it should be placed thusly: the deacon wraps the Cross in a cloth and carries it to that spot, singing the antiphons from Psalm 4:9, Psalm 15:9, Matthew 27:66. When the Cross is placed there, in burial style, they sing the antiphon: when the Lord was buried...' Then in imitation of the guards guiding the Lord's tomb, the monks shall keep watch during the night reverently chanting psalms.

The Good Friday ceremony is rather bare in essentials. Nevertheless what can be reconstructed is the element of drama, which supported its structure. To clarify this aspect, one could view it as:

Stage   Altar
Curtain   Altar curtain
Actors   Deacons

Script	Scriptural texts from Old and New Testaments
Chorus	Nocturnal Psalm chanting
Dramatization	Enactment of Christ's burial

5) *Holy Saturday*

This selection is very famous because it contains the *Quem quaeritis* selection. It reads:

> While the third lesson is being changed, let four monks vest themselves; one with an alb who approaches the place of the tomb, and there holding a palm in his hand sits down quietly. During the third responsory the other three monks vested in copes and carrying incense filled thuribles follow slowly, in a way as they are looking for something (pedetemptim). All this is done in imitation (imitationem) of the angel at the tomb and of the three Marys who carrying spices came to anoint the body of Jesus (Luke 23:54). When the seated one (angel) catches sight of the three others straying about, as if looking for something, approaches him and (with the directive) begins in a sweet voice of medium pitch:
>> "whom do you seek at the tomb?
>> Quem quaeritis...?"

The three respond in unison:

> "Jesus of Nazareth who was crucified."

The seated one then replies:

> "He is not here, He is risen as He said.
> Go, announce that He is risen from the dead."

At this, the three turn to the choir, (entrance of chancel) and say:

> Alleluia! The Lord is risen!

The one seated then sings:

128

Come and see the place where the Lord was laid. Alleluia, Alleluia!

While saying this, let him lift the veil and show them the place —
bare of the cross but only the cloth laid there with which the cross was
wrapped. The three place their thuribles aside and take the cloth and
hold it up before the clergy, as though showing them evidence that the
Lord is risen and no longer in the tomb, the antiphon is sung:

"Surrexit Dominus de sepulchro..."
The Lord is risen from the tomb, who for us hung upon the cross.

The cloth is then placed upon the altar. The *Te Deum* is sung and
the bells chime out together.[126]

The presentation is definitely acting rather than mimic impersona-
tion. The costumes worn are ecclesiastical vestments. The three Marys
wear copes and carry thuribles not spices as mentioned in the Gospels.
One notices the historical scene of the Gospel and this presentation.
The mystery is celebrated in a more public manner, the winding of the
cloth placed upon the altar, the actors as both play and office singers
and in a single communal chant of joy — *Te Deum*. The bells ring out
their Easter joy beyond the walls of the monastery. All contribute to a
dramatic effect, not only for the monks within the choir, but also for
the faithful beyond the chancel.

C.   *The Monastic Constitutions of Lanfranc — Decreta Lanfranci*

Lanfranc was born in Pavia, Italy in 1005 and served as Archbishop of
Canterbury from 1070 to 1089, the year of his death. It was during this time
that Lanfranc was the aide to William the Conqueror and was instrumental in
establishing harmonious relations between church and state after the Norman
Conquest. His influence was certainly felt in the reorganization of the church
and monasteries. This document (DL) reveals much Norman influence
because Lanfranc, as archbishop, resolved to reform his territory after the
Norman model. The monks conducted the services in the Cathedrals; Nor-

---

[126]   Dom Thomas Symons, *Regularis Concordia* (Thomas Nelson and Sons
Ltd., 1953), pp. 30-50.

man model. The monks conducted the services in the Cathedrals; Norman monasticism, moreover, offered its own peculiarities, its specific differences rising from the racial and cultural elements. One reads of the added richness in the ceremonies.

1. *Christmas Night*

All the bells are rung before the office begins. Four monks in copes sing the invitatory (Psalm 94).

In each nocturn at the third lesson, two priests in copes incense the main altar then the other monks in choir.

In the third nocturn the following Gospels are read: Matthew 1:1, Luke 2:15, John 1:1.

The Abbot begins the *Te Deum*. After this is read the geneology account of Jesus Christ. The antiphon is begun and the monks proceed to the Lady altar for Lauds....

After this the monks proceed into the church, the celebrant and ministers vest for Mass: the deacon in a dalmatic, two sub deacons in tunicles...for the responsory and the alleluia there shall be as many chanters as ordered and they are to be in copes.

At the pealing of the bells, the Mass begins.

2. *First Sunday of Lent*

After Compline a curtain is hung between the choir and the altar...the crucifix, reliquaries, and gospel books with images upon them, shall be covered.

The covering in the sanctuary would certainly evoke a powerful dramatic overtone. The intended sense of separation and penance created by the curtain aids in building a sense of conflict, so that at the Easter Vigil the catharsis is attained and salvation is won.

3. Palm Sunday

Blessing

At the end of terce, the gospel Turba Multa (Matt. 21:8) was read. Then the Abbot approaches and blesses the palms and flowers and other branches which are on the carpet before the main altar. They are blessed with holy water and incense.

Distribution

While the chanter sings the antiphon, Pueri Hebraeorum, the sacristans distribute the palms to the Abbot, prior....

Procession

The bells are rung, the banners are borne, lighted candles are at hand and the procession begins. Incense is also used in the procession. The Gospel books are carried by two subdeacons, after them come the monks then Abbot, who walks last. Various antiphons are sung during the procession. Now when the procession arrives at a certain point, they all halt and two priests dressed in albs, carry a shrine (ferestrum) in which the Host should be placed...the choir repeats the antiphon "Hosanna filio David".

The Abbot soon intones the antiphon "Ave, rex noster" (Hail our King)...all who pass the shrine genuflect.

When they arrive at the gates of the city, they halt forming two ranks with enough space between as the place allows, both sides then face the shrine in their midst. The gateway under which they processed through should be decorated with curtains and other hangings.

The chanter intones the *Gloria, laus* and the choir answers: *Israel es tu rex* and *Cui puerile decus* — the chanter then intones *Ingrediente Domino* as the procession enters the city...then the antiphon *Princepes sacerdotum* is sung as all enter the church.

Mass — There four monks in copes begin the antiphon

Circumdederunt me, and the Mass begins, while the bells are ringing.

What one sees here is the dramatic representation of the Lord's entry into Jerusalem. The action is supported by the Scriptures, Matthew 1: 1-17, John 22:12.

The whole community walks in procession with chants to a chosen spot outside the walls of the city where a halt is made before the shrine containing the Host.

The monks represent the crowd. All move back to the gate of the city, representing the gates of Jerusalem, here another stop is made. All move now to the main door of the church, where another stop is made, and chants recall the incidents of Caiaphas and the Pharisees. When all enter the church, a final stop is made before the crucifix at the entry to the choir. The feature of these 'stops' in the procession probably originated in Normandy. Later this usage would serve as a model for the procession on Corpus Christi.

Again one reads of text, action and participants all enchancing a dramatic whole.

4) *Tenebrae Service*

For the evening Office of Thursday (the Wednesday night before Holy Thursday) candles are lighted before the altar according to the number of antiphons and responsories which are sung. Prayers are said silently, then at the Our Father, the monks are to bow as much as they can over their place in the choir stall...at every antiphon and every responsory a candle shall be extinguished. After the Lamentations and other prayers, all the candles are distinguished in the whole church except one, which burns in the choir area until the antiphon *Traditor autem* is sung.

This impressive service gets its name from the first word of the first antiphon used at the beginning — "Tenebrae factae sunt" — Darkness.....If there were antithesis to the ceremony of Lighting the Lights, this rite could be its total opposite and termed "The Extinguishing of the Lights". What makes this ceremony so moving is the gradual moving toward the total effect that darkness has over the whole community. Granted that the symbolism of darkness was taken into consideration, the dramatic setting brings this across more vividly. The candles are lighted on a huge stand:

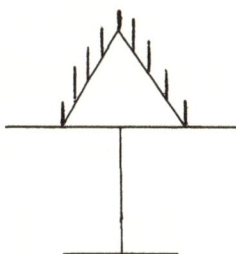

As the psalms and antiphons are completed, a candle is extinguished, until the middle candle symbolizing Christ, is removed and hidden during the *Benedictus* at Lauds. It is brought out at the end of the office and only then is it extinguished. The chanting is very solemn and unflowery. Somberness pervades. The church is now in total darkness. This is how the Triduum of the Lord's Passion and Death begins. The atmosphere will give way to that of a womb at the Easter Vigil when the Light (Pascal Candle) will be blessed and once again the whole church will be radiant in light — a surely dramatic tone in which the Resurrection of the life-giving Lord is commemorated.

5. *Easter Vigil*

The blessing of the Pascal candle deserves attention here.

"...the deacon receives the thurible and incenses the candle. The sacristan lights the candle as soon as the words are reached: 'Rutilans ignis accendit—'

...The candle remains lighted until next day's Vespers.

At the end of the Litany, the leaders of song sing in a loud voice 'Kindle the lights', three times. At this point the candles are lighted throughout the church; the *Kyrie* is sung in a festal tone, the priest approaches the altar with the procession and the bells are kept ringing until the end of the *Kyrie*. Copes are distributed to those who will sing the Alleluia.

133

Again there are overwhelming voices, lights, costumes and directives which serve as contributing factors that dramatically impresses the congregation. One must keep in mind that the Pascal candle was extremely huge — of a human size, and sometimes standing as high as thirty feet. At times, the difficulty of lighting it caused the introduction of various means, similar to ladders and pulleys, which facilitated its lighting by the deacon or other ministers.

One can only imagine how impressive this synbol of Christ really was. The date which was inscribed, and the placing of a cross with grains of incense commemorating the five wounds of Christ were in full view of the congregation:

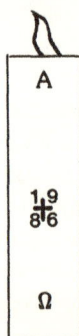

The next impressive rite was the singing of the *Exultet* by the deacon, while the Pascal Candle was ablaze beside him at the pulpit. The beautiful chant was written on a scroll so that as the *Exultet* was sung, the scroll was unwound over the pulpit, the congregation would then behold lavishly painted portrayals of religious scenes — a mere delight for the congregation! This bit of information sounds so familiar in essence with modern day audiovisual techniques.

6.   *Reception of Monastic Visitors*

In his reforms, Lanfranc seems to have covered all aspects of life which would influence monastery life. In this simple but impressive rite, a visitor is greeted with much impressive and dramatic nuances. Lanfranc gives directives:

"Receive the visitor with a solemn procession...a carpet is prepared on the top step before the main altar.

At the reception, the Abbot sprinkles the visitor with holy water, incense is offered and the gospel book is presented. The bells are ringing all this while.

The leader of song chants a hymn or psalm suitable to the visitor; the procession then returns...upon reaching the altar, the visitor kneels in prayer. Later the visitor is led to the chapter room, where he reads a passage from Scripture and gives a homily...He greets the monks at a convenient time."[127]

D. *St. Hildegard of Bingen* — 1098-1179 A.D.

St. Hildegard wrote her private revelations and expository works on the gospel as well as lives of local saints, together with poems and hymns for the edification of those who believed in her claim as a mystic. It is among these writings, that a play *Ordo Virtutem* is found.[128] Peter Dronke maintains that this play is "by more than a century our earliest surviving morality play".[129] The story is rather unpredictable while the characters Anima, Diabolus and Virtutes are personifications; this allows the dramatic action to revolve around their specific traits. As a result, there is present a dramatic tension, and sudden moments of dramatic irony. A look at the play would be interesting,

---

[127] David Knowles. *The Monastic Constitutions of Lanfranc,* (Thomas Nelson & Sons, Ltd.), New York City, New York, 1951.

[128] Two other interesting writers of this era are Hroswitha (c. 960 A.D.) and Hilarius (c. 1125 A.D.). Hroswitha wrote six *comediae* in praise of virtue, her plays lack stage directions. Humor and buffoonery are focus in *Dulcitius*, while maintaining the tone that the efforts of evil amount to naught and virtue is the long run triumphs. Her genius is evident, for she formulates secular feelings into sacred ones, and transforms her pagan models into Christian ones. *Gallicanus* is equally interesting, written in an allegorical style, the plot surrounds the conversion of the Emperor's servant to Christianity. Hilarius was probably an Englishman, who studied under Abelard. His three plays are *Raising of Lazarus; ...Life of St. Nicholas;* and *Prophet Daniel.* All these works lack musical notations. Richard Axton, *European Drama of Early Middle Ages:* Hutchinson University Library, London, England, 1974.

[129] Peter Dronke. *Poetic Individuality in the Middle Ages,* Claredon Press, Oxford, England, 1970, p. 169.

135

Prologue

The *Patriarchs and Prophets sings*:
Who are there, who are like the clouds? of Isaiah 60:8

The *Virtutes* answer:
You holy ones of old, why do you marvel at us? The Word of
God is bright in the shape of man, and so we shine with him, building
up the members of his beautiful body.

Soon the devil speaks, his chains clank and he speaks to Anima:
"What's the use of hard effort, foolish, foolish? Look to the world
— it will embrace with great honor."

A long lyrical selection follows in which the Virtues dance, each in turn is
soloist, introducing herself and calling the others into a circle about her in
token of their own coronation, i.e. their perseverance. Note its similarity to
Ausonius' work above.

"...I am Humanity, queen of Virtues, I say: Come to me, and I will
feed you...."

The other virtues sing in chorus:
"O glorious queen and most sweet mediatrix we are coming to
you freely."

Caritas joins in:
"I am Charity, a lovely flower — come to me, Virtues, and I will
lead you into the clear light of the flower upon the branch."

The devil continues here with his mocking interruptions and demands:
"Where is your champion?"

The virtues sing of the joy of the heavenly kingdom and of the em-
braces of the royal bridegroom.
"O, Virginity, you are in the royal bedchamber.
O, how sweetly you shine in the King's embrace..."

While this is going on, beyond the circle is the devil, wolf-like In search of his prey — tender sheep in a pastoral paradise.

They are warned by the virtue Innocence:
"Run away, O sheep, from the devil's foul play!"

They in turn answer:
Let us flee running to your aid."

What is interesting to note here is the performance of the dance. This dance of God's followers is the counterpart to the dance of love in which the chorus sings of love's mystery. The idea of redemption is celebrated, the voice of the Creator:

"In mente altissimi, O Satana, caput tuum conculcavi..."
"In the mind of the Most High, O Satan, I trampled on your head and in the virgin I nurtured a sweet miracle, know let all who dwell in heaven rejoice..."

There is almost a tint of a "gamos" in this section. Moreover, the end seems to have an epilogue:

"So now, all you people,
kneel before your Father
so that He may stretch out
His hand to you."

This ending, together with the Gregorian style music and symbolic staging would indicate that the performance was located in a liturgical setting. It is in this regard, that Hildegard changes secular forms into sacred forms; again, she handles the blending of earthly and heavenly love rather artistically despite the mystical overtone.[130] Hildegard's work was surely a thrust which brought the dramatic activity of the Middle Ages to a fuller appreciation.

---

[130] Richard Axton, European Drama of the Early Middle Ages, pp. 94-99. Peter Dronke, *Poetic Individuality in the Middle Ages*, pp. 169-179.

E. *Monastic Displeasure*

Aelred of Rievaulx (1109-1167 A.D.), a contemporary of Hildegard, entered the monastic life at the age of twenty. In his work *Mirror of Charity*, he attempts to reform various abuses that could easily creep into monastic worship. One would find these observations rather amusing and informative:

> "...I shall consider those who use religion as a pretext for justifying the pleasures which our ears may enjoy...once musical instruments were allowed, now the Church has outgrown the stage... what are we doing, I often wonder, with the thunder of organ music, the clash of cymbals and the elaborate part-setting for different voices? One hears of monks doing all sorts of things with their voices, some sound like lady of falsettos, others like bleating, and tremalos."

> He continues to mention his own awareness of some monks who sing with their mouths opened, as though they are grasping for air in their last hour, some look as though they were lost in rapture during the service.

> He says some monks wave their arms about, keeping time to the music and twisting with their bodies in all directions. They do this in the name of religion, and because this is done, they think they praise God more — "et ubi haec frquentius agitantur, ibi Deo honorabilius serviri clamatur."

> "Moreover the simple folk", he continues, "may be impressed by the organ music, but they cannot help laughing at the ridiculous show in the choir. They think they are more at a theatre watching a show than praying in church — "ut eos non ad oratorium sed ad theatrum, nec ad orandum sed ad spectandum..."

> "The one time practices of devotion become excuses for frivolous pleasure, the music is preferred rather than the meaning of the sung words..."[131]

---

[131] PL 195:571. St. Aelred of Rieaulx, *The Mirror of Charity*, The Catholic Book Club, 121 Charing Cross Road, London, England, 1962, pp. 72-73.

Monasticism, however, did give the church, besides the Divine Office, the concepts that work too is a prayer and that worship is not some private section of one's life. The Eucharist was the center and pivot of daily life, indeed the benefit of that interplay between the secular and the monastic elements in the church never ceased to enrich and strengthen devotion in different ways and at different times, as was shown above. The external beauty of the ritual, undoubtedly evoked the sentiment that worship is the ultimate end of man's activity. Through ritual and symbol gesture, the monk brought this great balancing element to Christian public worship.[132]

[132]Dom Gregory Dix, *The Shape of Liturgy*, (Dacre Press, Westminster, England, 1954) pp. 330-332.

IX
Sundry Elements of Dramatic Nature in the Liturgy

A. *Eastern Testimony*
1. *Narsai of Edessa* — (ob. 503 A.D.)

In his homily XVII, Narsai gives the detailed outline of ritual with its dramatic nuances found in the Eucharistic Celebration in use at his time. Although he interprets the gestures symbolically, nevertheless he mentions the various rites which afford this work with enough information so that the reader may become aware of the ceremonies which contain latent seed of dramatic expression.

Homily XVII

> ...The priests assemble in the sanctuary, they bar the image of the Apostles who met together at the Lord's tomb.

> ...The altar is a symbol of the Lord's tomb, the veil which is over the gifts is a type of the stone that sealed the tomb...

> ...The deacons standing on each side brandishing the fans are symbolic of the angels who sat at the edge of the Lord's tomb. All the other deacons who stand before the altar depict a likeness of the angels who

surrounded the Lord's tomb. The sanctuary is symbolic of the Garden whence flowered life for all mankind.

...The priest's voice now admonishes everyone to confess to the Lord:
"Give heed and look with your minds
    on what is being done.
    "Pray with the priest:
    Bend to the ground the eye's glances and stretch to the heights
    the glances of the mind..."

The priest uncovers the gifts and casts on one side the veil that was covering them; he cries out:
    "Look upon Him who is not mystically slain on the altar."

The people answer:
    "We lift our minds to you, O Lord."

The priest cries out:
    "This acceptable and pure oblation is offered to the Lord,

The people answer:
    "It is meet and worth to offer this oblation for all."

...In all silence the altar stands crowned with beauty and splendor...the Gifts are set in order, the censers are smoking, the lights are shining and the deacons are hovering and whisking the fans...silence overwhelms the whole area...The bright robed priest recounts the glorious deeds of God, the people answer:
    "Holy, Holy, Holy Lord..."

...The priest stands at the door and stretches his hands to bless the people and says:
    "He that blessed us, may He also bless us with the power of His mysteries."

With his right hand, the bright robed priest confers his blessing on the assembly...[133]

---

[133]   Dom R. H. Connolly, *Liturgical Homilies of Narsai*, Cambridge University

It is quite evident that the homily gives enough material to visualize the dramatic elements contained in the liturgy as viewed and recorded by Narsai. To facilitate the image, one may view it as:

Homily XVII	*Dramatic Elements*
Stage Area	Sanctuary
Stage Properties	Sanctuary accessories: door, altar veil, lights, censer, gifts.
Actors	Priests, deacons
Costume	Vestments
Spectators	Assembly
Dialogue, Texts	Scriptural selections, Prayers, partial participation, singing
Action	Bowing, moving about, carrying lights, hand motion: raising, extending...

B. *Western Testimony*
1) *Gregory of Tours* (ob 594 A.D.)

In his work History of the Franks, Gregory describes the baptism of Clovis (Book II, Chapter 31) in very similar terms used by Narsai:

"Remi, the bishop of Rheims was delighted to hear that Clovis was ready to be accepted into the Christian family...the city square were shaded with tapestried canopies, the churches adorned with white curtains, the baptistry was prepared. The aroma of incense spread about, candles, too, emitted a fragrant odor and burned brightly, the interior of the church was filled with a divine fragrance, the bishop told Clovis, as he entered the baptistry:

"Bend your neck, worship what you burned, burn what you worshipped."

And so the king believed in the Trinity ...and was anointed with holy Chrism...[134]

Press, England, 1909.
[134] PL 71:226.

2) *Diocese of Monza* — Northern Italy

An interesting rite takes place in the Liturgy of Good Friday. At the conclusion of Solemn Prayers, three servers receive a chest (archa) covered with a cloth on which lies the Gospel Book, a large paten and a cross adorned with gems. This ark is led in procession to the steps of the altar while an antiphon is sung. The Lenten veil is lifted and the procession proceeds to the corner of the altar while *Polule meus* is sung. When this is completed, the ark is taken behind the altar — two servers sing the *Trisagion* to which the choir replies:

Servers:	Agios O Theos
Choir:	Sanctus Deus — Holy God
Servers:	Agios Ischyros
Choir:	Sanctus Fortis — Holy Mighty One
Servers:	Agios athanatos, eleison imas
Choir:	Sanctus Inmortalis — Holy Immortal One
	Miserere nobis — have mercy on us.

At its conclusion, the veil is raised and they proceed with the Ark into the choir while the hymn *Ecce lignum* is sung. The Ark is placed on a carpet during the singing of another hymn, after which the clergy kiss the cross and the rite of Communion follows.[135] The *Trisagion* is so similar to the chorus used in classical drama, by which the emotions of the assembly are conveyed. Another interesting observation would be the withdrawal of the Ark from the spectator's view thus intensifying emotion as well.

3. *Diocese of Milan* — Northern Italy

The preparatory act of covering the altar with a cloth is attested to by early church writers (Optatus of Milevis and Theodore of Mopsuestia). Soon this rite received various symbolic interpretations. It was likened to the grave

---

[135] PL Archdale A. King, *Liturgies of the Past*, (Longmans, Green and Co. Ltd., London, England, 1959), pp. 47-49.

cloths of Jesus.[136] For all practical purposes, this use of the cloth served a very elementary need — to cover the altar and to serve as a cloth to receive any crumbs which might flake off from the consecrated Loaf, for Christ is truly present, even in tiny bread fragments. The Church usage in Milan composed prayers according to various feasts for this rite of 'spreading the tablecloth.' Here, again text and action in a liturgical setting afford an outlet for dramatic expression. The text treats of the feast being celebrated: for Epiphany one reads:

Oratio super sindonem	*Prayer over the Cloth*
Tribue, quaesumus, omnipotens Deus ut sicut omnes nationes veniunt...	Grant, O God, that as all nations joyfully came to adore Your Son, Christ the Lord, so now may that light (Christ) which guided the Magi, shine in us...

For the feast of St. Ambrose, December 6:

Exaudi, Domine, preces nostras, etc...	Hear our prayers, O Lord, and free us from all harm by your protection, through the prayers of St. Ambrose...

The prayer for the Sunday after the feast of St. John the Baptist's beheading reads as follows:

"O Lord, you see how we are not able to endure the many dangers our weak humanity causes us, grant us health of mind and body so that we may override those things we suffer due to our sins, with your help we will come out strong. We ask this of You through Jesus Christ, Our Lord..."

4. *Diocese of Toledo*

From the earliest times, the celebration of the Eucharist contained the element of breaking the consecrated Bread, in imitation of the Lord's action performed at the Last Supper.[137] He gave Himself to His Apostles by giving them His body from the one loaf. This breaking of Bread became the climax in the primitive church, indeed, its very name — 'Fractio Panis' became the term to describe the Eucharistic rite itself.

Various ceremonies eventually surrounded this sacred rite. One such elaborate ceremony is recorded in the liturgy of the Church of Toledo, also known as the Mozarabic Rite.

a) *Breaking of Bread*

The rite consists of the arranging of the Host particles in the form of a cross on the paten. The Host is divided in the middle, the one half is placed on the paten while the other half is divided into five parts. The first half is then divided into four parts. Each broken part is referred to a mystery in the life of the Lord. This is mentioned as the particles are broken. The nine parts are then arranged in the form of a cross:

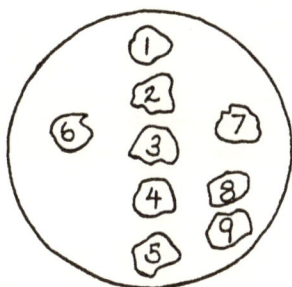

1. Incarnation
2. Birth
3. Circumcision
4. Epiphany
5. Passion
6. Death
7. Resurrection
8. Glory
9. Kingdom

The symbolism of the arrangement speaks for itself, the Incarnation is the beginning of salvation, the Glory and Kingdom represent Christ as conqueror of death and sin, and the fact that He is seated at the right hand of the Father.

The celebrant continues by washing his hands and covering the chalice.[138] Here text and action blend into a dramatic whole.

---

[137] Luke 24:30, Acts 2:42, *Didache* IX, 3.
[138] Archdale King. *Liturgies of the Primatial Sees* (Bruce Publishing Co., Milwaukee, Wisconsin, 1957), pp. 615-617.

Another interesting feature containing a dramatic overtone in the same liturgy is the section called the *Missa*. This selection of prayer and words has a dramatic potential, insofar that it can evoke the mood or tone of the feast being celebrated. The nature of this section is very similar to that of a dramatic prologue.

The prayer itself was constructed in two parts. The first part will be noted below for it is directed to the congregation, while the other part is directed to God. This prayer had the function of emphasizing the special liturgical character of the day.

Sample texts will manifest the potential of highlighting the particular feast:

Christmas
> "Now is the acceptable time; today salvation is ours,
> Let us walk in light, the Redeemer has appeared...
> The living bread is given to believers...
> The font is gushing forth for believers...
> He gives us life; He will die for us.
> He causes our being...
> May we be given His grace and mercy.

Tuesday in Holy Week
> "Dearly beloved, we are bound to entreat Him by our prayers and to do penance by our tears, while offering the living sacrifice to our most loving God...Let us serve Him by fasting and contrition of heart, so that He may cleanse our flesh and arouse our dull minds to love Him...."

Holy Thursday
> "Let us choose and follow justice, dearly beloved, desiring to eat at the Lord's supper.
> Let no one approach with unworthy thoughts...
> Let us all imitate the suffering of the Lord...
> Let us imitate the His humility, as expressed when He washed His disciples feet.
> Let us imitate His goodness which was denied by Peter...."

Fifth Sunday after Easter
> "This is the day which the Lord has made....